INTRODUCTION

Above all, the sixties was a decade of excitement. It was the decade when
to blow away the clouds of austerity that had cloaked post war Britain for fifteen long years.

The baby boom of the late forties became the teenage boom of the early to mid sixties and with it a youth culture whose double mission appeared to be to break down class barriers and to display an irreverence towards established institutions and what was perceived as their out of date values.

The decade will forever be immortalised in the history books as the swinging sixties and few of us old enough to remember can resist the temptation to look back with pleasant nostalgia at the pop music revolution, the flamboyant new fashions, the hippies, the summer of love or the new found sexual freedom as a result of The Pill.

However, let us not forget that the sixties was also a decade of unrest. Against the backdrop of all that epitomized the spirit of the swinging sixties, there was the constant threat of nuclear war. The crisis in Cuba, civil war in Africa, the Russian invasion of Czechoslovakia, unrest in the Middle East and the Vietnam War all dominated world headlines during the sixties.

In Sunderland, as we moved out of the fifties and into the sixties, there was every reason to feel optimistic about life. Unemployment, the scourge of subsequent decades, was a statistic suffered by an unfortunate minority and ambitious slum clearance projects meant that living standards for many Wearsiders rapidly improved as new houses with all mod cons were built on the newly cleared sites.

Plans for a new town centre shopping area were entering the construction stage which, when complete, would propel Sunderland into the forefront of modern shopping environments while a plethora of night clubs, restaurants, dance halls and fashion shops appeared to open overnight to ensure that there was an abundance of leisure activites for the young and the young at heart.

SUNDERLAND IN THE SIXTIES journeys down memory lane year by year and, in doing so, it will hopefully bring back some vivid recollections of events experienced by those of us old enough to remember those halcyon days, long gone.

Those not old enough to remember might just have one or two regrets at missing out on that unique blend of excitement that was essentially the sixties.

Flyleaf Caption

Bygone Sunderland. This 1962 photograph of Fawcett Street shows three aspects of Sunderland which are no longer with us. The majestic Town Hall towers over other buildings in the street while Binns stores on the east and west side of the street sold goods for the most discerning of customers. Two buses from the Sunderland Corporation fleet stir fond memories of the days when the town council could boast its own transport department.

THE SUNDERLAND ECHO

The Sunderland Echo story began in 1873 with the publication of the first edition of the Sunderland Daily Echo which was founded by Samuel Storey, great grandfather of the present chairman, Sir Richard Storey. Until then, Sunderland had been served by two weekly newspapers, the Sunderland Times and Sunderland Herald but for daily news, Sunderland people relied largely upon newspapers published in Newcastle and South Shields.

From relatively humble beginnings in Press Lane, off High Street in Sunderland, the Sunderland Daily Echo was launched on an initial investment of £3,500 to provide the expanding town with its first daily evening newspaper. The future prosperity of the newspaper was assured when new premises were opened in Bridge Street where new print presses provided greatly increased capacity.

Samuel Storey was elected Mayor of Sunderland in 1876 and the town's MP in 1881. Soon afterwards, he teamed up with Scottish born American millionaire Andrew Carnegie to form a newspaper syndicate to start up new titles and to acquire existing ones. Included in these titles were the Portsmouth Evening News and the Northern Daily Mail in Hartlepool.

In 1885, the syndicate broke up but Samuel Storey retained his interests in the Sunderland Echo, the Portsmouth Evening News and the Northern Daily Mail (which in 1959 was renamed The Mail) and in 1934 the three titles were brought together as Portsmouth and Sunderland Newspapers Limited.

In 1976, The Sunderland Echo moved from its Bridge Street site to new purpose built premises at Pennywell while 1987 saw re-organisation within the group and the creation of subsidiary companies for the northern and southern publishing and printing organisations. At that time, the Sunderland Echo became part of Sunderland and Hartlepool Publishing and Printing Limited.

During 1991, Sunderland and Hartlepool Publishing and Printing Limited acquired the interest of two of Britain's oldest newspaper publishing companies; The Northern Press and Northern Gazette Limited. Northeast Press was born out of the amalgamation of the three companies.

At the cutting edge of newspaper technology throughout its long and distinguished history, the Sunderland Echo is today one of the country's major evening newspapers, produced by the latest computerised typesetting and web offset colour printing techniques.

The Sunderland Echo is a high quality newspaper produced to provide the Wearside area with a service which informs, educates and entertains as well as adding to and protecting the quality of local life.

Mel Kirtley
1995.

Sunderland Echo & Shipping Gazette Thursday, January 28, 1960

Echo
SUNDERLAND

No. 27,487 (87th YEAR)   TWOPENCE HALFPENNY
THURSDAY, JANUARY 28, 1960

SIX O'CLOCK

1960

SHIPYARD WAGE CLAIM PROMISE

Employers To Consider Renewed Plea

THE shipbuilding employers in London today promised to consider the renewed claims for a substantial wage increase and a 40-hour week for 200,000 in the industry. Representatives of the Confederation of Shipbuilding and Engineering Unions were told this by the Shipbuilding Employers' Federaton.

The claims were rejected on November 18 but the employers told the unions that, if they co-operated in removing obstacles to maximum efficiency, they could achieve some reduction in hours without increased costs.

As in the case of general engineering, the unions decided to try again. On Tuesday, the engineering employers again refused to grant a wage increase but offered a 42-hour week, compared with their previous offer of 42 and a half hours.

This was not accepted by the unions and they will meet at York on February 11 to decide the next step.

Few Orders

Mr G. Harold R. Towers, chairman and managing director of John Readhead and Sons Ltd., South Shields, and president of the Shipbuilding Employers' Federation, replying today to the shipyard claim pointed out that there had been no real change in the condition of the industry since the last meeting.

The very few orders taken had all been secured in the face of the keenest competition and at very low and unremunerative fixed prices in the interests of shipyard production programmes and of maintaining employment.

The position on repair work was very much the same. Prospects, therefore, were not any brighter.

Mr Towers said he had made it perfectly clear when they last met that in view of the unfavourable outlook for both shipbuilding and ship-repairing all their efforts must be directed towards reducing their prices and they could not, therefore, agree to increased wages.

Not Opposed

So far as working hours were concerned the employers had stated that they were not opposed in principle to a reduction, but it was absolutely essential before any such claim was considered that the obstacles to maximum efficiency should be removed.

At the previous conference the employers had said that if the unions were prepared to co-operate with them they might still be able to do something to meet the claim for shorter hours, but it would be dishonest to suggest that without that co-operation the industry could face up to a reduction in hours at the present time when the position was so grave.

Problems

"That is still our position," declared Mr Towers. "It now appears that you wish us to go back to our constituents and we will take immediate steps to do so.

"We should, however, like to be in a position, when taking

Continued in Page 6.

30,000 Fowls Die In Blaze

OVER 30,000 chickens were lost in a blaze today which badly damaged a five-storey mill near Elland, Yorks., used for rearing broilers.

No Change

TODAY'S bulletin on Mr Aneurin Bevan at the Royal Free Hospital, London, stated that there was no change in his condition. His four doctors saw him again today. Yesterday his condition was said to have shown some improvement.

The outbreak started on the fourth floor and flames shot 100 feet into the air as 100 firemen from seven areas fought the flames.

Another section of the mill, used by a firm of animal foodstuff manufacturers and containing machinery and stock worth nearly £40,000, was saved.

ONE SURVIVOR

People living next to the mill were warned to be ready to leave their homes. Two hours after the outbreak started, sections of the 80-foot walls fell, blocking the road.

Only one chicken survived. It ran out when the firemen arrived and forced an entry.

French Police In Crisis Raids

FRENCH police today raided the homes of extreme right wing politicians in Paris and provincial cities as some 6,000 insurrectionists in Algiers continued to defy President de Gaulle's Algerian policy.

Almost simultaneously the Algerian authorities raised the censorship clamped down four days ago after bloody rioting toured off the present crisis.

GENERAL ARRESTED

The police raids in France were part of a magistrate's inquiry into "attempts against the internal authority of the state."

Some documents were seized and a right-wing deputy, Jean Marie Le Pen, leader of the National Combatants' Front was arrested.

Some of those arrested have already been released, including retired Air Force General Lionel Chassin, former commander of NATO's Central Europe Air Defence.

INSULTING REMARKS

Police said the raids were aimed at people who had signed leaflets distributed in the last few days and containing insulting remarks against de Gaulle.

In the first uncensored dispatch from the North African capital, it was reported that the insurrectionists were firmly entrenched behind their barricades with vast quantities of arms and ammunition.

Several thousand Europeans massed outside the Casbah in a bid to capture the atmosphere of fraternity which marked the first settlers' revolt in 1958 which brought de Gaulle to power.

DOWN MINE

MR MACMILLAN today put on heavy boots, overalls, and a miner's helmet to go 4,000 feet underground into the West Driefontein mine — one of the richest gold mines in the world. He took a keen interest in a rock-breaking machine and Africans operating pneumatic rock drills.

SHOPS PLAN FOR CINEMA

The Gaumont Cinema in Sunderland—a familiar landmark in the town—may close. See story below.   —S.E.

The Gaumont May Close

SUNDERLAND Corporation Planning Committee has approved plans for the conversion of the Gaumont Cinema, Fawcett Street,—the first cinema to show "talkies" in the town—into shops and offices. But a spokesman for the Rank Organization, owners of the property, said today; "We have no immediate plans for closing the cinema."

The cinema was opened in December, 1915, and was then named the Havelock. It was owned at that time by Provincial Cinematograph Theatres Ltd, but in 1930 it went over to Gaumont British and 18 years late was absorbed into the Rank Organization.

will be asked to approve the plans at its next meeting.

The Rank spokesman said that negotiations were at present taking place for the sale of the property and that no decision about the closure of the cinema would be made until the sale had been completed.

SURPRISE TO HIM

It stands on the site of the old Havelock House, one of Sunderland's major stores until it was destroyed in 1898 in the worst fire in the history of the town.

There have been no structural alterations since it opened. The cinema was the first to show "talkie" films in Sunderland on July 15, 1929. Within the last 12 months it has been redecorated. It has always kept in line with the times, adopting each new method as it came along including stereophonic sound and the broad screen.

When told about the plans, the manager, Mr H. Minnican, replied: "The news has knocked me off my chair."

Sunderland Town Council

He Has Lost The Chance Of Promotion

£5,250 DAMAGES FOR ENGINEER

A 37-YEAR-OLD I.C.I. plant engineer, who had lost the chance of promotion and could not enjoy his hobbies because of injuries received in a crash between two buses was awarded £5,250 damages, with costs, at Durham Assizes today.

Norman Henry Harvey, of Guisborough Road, Middlesbrough, heard Mr Justice Edmund Davies say that in consequence of his injuries he was entitled to substantial damages. He had worked for I.C.I. as a plant engineer for 19 years and had excellent prospects.

HIS GREAT INTEREST

The theatre was his great interest but now he could no longer go because of his discomfort of sitting for any length of time. He could not follow his hobbies of gardening and sport which he had enjoyed before the accident.

Mr Stanley Price, Q.C., for Harvey, had said that two people were killed and 30 injured in the crash between two buses owned by United Automobile Services Ltd., Darlington, who admitted liability.

Mr Harvey's pelvis was fractured and he now suffered from a large measure of permanent disability and pain, said Mr Price. The pain was becoming intolerable.

TRANSFERRED

He could no longer do his former job in the I.C.I.'s new five-floor synthetic rubber plant because of the amount of stair climbing involved and he had been transferred to the Perspex factory.

Greed The Motive For Brutal Murder Of Man, Jury Told

GREED was probably the primary motive in the mind of John George Bates (29), of no fixed address, when he brutally murdered a young West Hartlepool painter, alleged Mr A. B. Boyd, prosecuting at Durham Assizes today.

For, within 12 hours of the disappearance of the murdered man, Gordon Rayner, of South Parade, Bates, who had been a lodger at the house, started to sell his victim's clothes.

Bates pleaded not guilty to the capital murder of Rayner,

in furtherance of theft. He is alleged to have battered him to death with a hammer.

Some two or three months before the murder, said Mr Boyle, Bates had gone to live with Rayner, a single man, whose sister, Mrs Elsie Hope, had left the house after her marriage.

Rayner was last seen alive by his girl friend, Miss Lillian Noble, when he called at her house on November 2. He disappeared from the sight of his friends and relations until November 9 when his sister and a Miss Jean Blenkinsopp discovered his body.

Mr Boyle told the jury: "The prosecution alleges that it was the hands of Bates which killed Rayner and probably his primary motive was greed, in that it was his intention to possess Gordon Rayner's property and house."

Within some 12 hours of Rayner's disappearance the prisoner got his mother to pawn for him a suit for 30s. That suit belonged to Rayner.

In the next seven days Bates took three men — Ronald Corbett, Tom Mincher, and John Davison to the house where Rayner's body lay.

[Proceeding]

This front page headline from The Sunderland Echo dated 28th January 1960 came as a shock to many Wearsiders. Sunderland Corporation Planning Committee had approved plans for the conversion of the Gaumont Cinema in Fawcett Street into shops and offices.

5

IT WAS IN 1960 ....

National Service ended

The farthing was withdrawn as legal currency

Penguin Books won the court case concerning Lady Chatterley's Lover. The Judge ruled that the book was not obscene and publication was permitted

Coronation Street was first transmitted

Traffic Wardens were introduced

The first bowling alley was opened in Britain

Ban The Bomb campaign was launched by CND supporters

A television licence cost £4

Tights first went on sale in Britain

The first MOT test certificates were issued

Z Cars, the most popular ever TV police series, was first shown

Looking High High High by Bryan Johnson was the UK entry in the Eurovision Song Contest. It was voted into second position

The Apartment won Best Picture category in Academy Awards

David Broome won BBC Sports Personality Of The Year

The first Motorway Service Area was opened at Newport Pagnell

The UK's first artificial ski slope was opened

The average annual wage for a manual worker was £282

Barbara Moore walked from Lands End to John O'Groats

Two dogs were returned alive from Space

200,000 people mostly skilled workers, left East Germany for West Germany

A single record cost 6s 8d, an EP cost 10s 9d and an LP cost £1 12s 6d

In Sunderland in 1960...

The central area of the town was designated the first smoke free area as part of Sunderland Corporation's long term programme 'to rid Sunderland of industrial smog.' Only authorised fuels were to be used in premises boarded by High Street West, Crowtree Road, West Park, Toward Road and Norfolk Street.

Hepworth & Grandage announced their intention to build a factory on a 20 acre site which would eventually employ 1000 men in the manufacture of piston and piston rings for the car industry. During the same week, Jackson The Taylor released plans to build a £300,000 factory in West Wear Street which would create 1000 jobs. The factory would be the company's third site in the town.

Archaeologists opened a mass grave in Sunderland and suggested that the scores of skeletons found were the remains of a massacre dating back to 875 when The Vikings invaded Sunderland.

The town centre's first one way traffic system was introduced for an experimental period of one month. Fawcett Street was reserved for north bound traffic while John Street carried only south bound vehicles.

An aerial view of High Street West in 1960 when two way traffic still ran the length of the street. The facade of the BHS store, seen here on the second block of buildings, was extensively updated later in the decade.

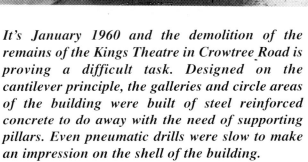

It's January 1960 and the demolition of the remains of the Kings Theatre in Crowtree Road is proving a difficult task. Designed on the cantilever principle, the galleries and circle areas of the building were built of steel reinforced concrete to do away with the need of supporting pillars. Even pneumatic drills were slow to make an impression on the shell of the building.

In 1960, a suit was an essential part of any fun loving holiday-maker's kit.

Sunderland Corporation Estates Committee recommended the transfer of tenants who persisted in neglecting their gardens to alternative accommodation without gardens. The Corporation's Best Kept Garden competition had been launched to encourage people to take a personal pride in their garden but it was reported that a small number of tenants persisted in neglect.

Sunderland Civic Theatre announced a trading loss of £23,830 for its first ten months of operation under Corporation management.

The unemployment figure of 4326 was the lowest recorded in Sunderland for two years.

The town's first free parking scheme was introduced at Park Lane and Tavistock Place. Attendants were employed during the first month of the scheme to assist motorists when parking their cars and to ensure that they did not cause an obstruction. However, once the attendants had finished work at 6.00pm, bogus personnel were found operating in the car park on more than one occasion, charging motorists for parking their cars.

Bridge Street South in 1960. A Morris Minor passes the former Sunderland Echo office as it heads towards Fawcett Street prior to the introduction of the one way traffic system.

First heard on the Telly.
It "caught on" in the home!
Now you hear it everywhere

I like JAM!

I like BUTTER!

I like CHEESE!

THICK TEA

Some folk like THICK TEA with jam or butter, others want them plain or with cheese, or honey. But they all agree about the biscuits. Wrights THICK TEA are big, crunchy, full of goodness and enjoyment. No wonder the North calls them a meal in a biscuit.

REGD. TRADE MARK

have you tried our **FIG ROLLS?**
Delicious figs wrapped in mouth-melting shortbread — a real tea-time treat.

WRIGHT'S
Biscuits Ltd. of South Shields

Whatever happened to Thick Tea Biscuits?

Bedford Street on a wet afternoon in 1960. South Pacific was showing at The Royal and a Sunderland Echo van heads into town with that day's edition.

A popular shopping area during the early sixties was The Arcade where Palmers store enjoyed a strong presence.

Broadway Secondary School was opened to cater for 320 of the town's 3200 pupils. The school took two years to build and was the third of its type in Sunderland; being similar in design to Farringdon and Castle View schools.

Plans to bring a casino to Seaburn were rejected outright by Sunderland Corportion Seaside Development Committee.

Sunderland Corporation applied to the Local Boundary Commission to increase the area of the town to more than double its present size while increasing the population by 50,000. Plans involved the annexing of the entire Sunderland Rural and Boldon Urban Districts in order to satisfy the need for extra land to meet housing, educational and industrial requirements.

Sunderland Corporation Planning Committee granted development approval for Binns to build a new store on the site of their former premises (which had been destroyed by enemy action during World War Two) at the junction of Fawcett Street and Borough Road. At the same meeting, plans were also approved for the conversion of the Gaumont Cinema in Fawcett Street into shops and offices.

Sixteen year old Dominic Sharkey made his first team debut for Sunderland in a Second Divison game against Scunthorpe United on April 9. Sunderland won 1-0 in front of a 16,952 crowd.

The Whitsuntide holiday saw the opening of Seaburn's new look holiday resort with Corporation staff ready to cope with the anticipated influx of 250,000 people, it was reported in The Sunderland Echo. 5000 new deck chairs and 300 beach huts were on hand for daily hire while a new £20,000 car park next to Seaburn Hall was prepared to receive 400 cars and 100 coaches. A newly installed £300 amplification system at various points along the promenade would be a boom to harassed parents of lost children.

Farringdon Social Club opened in December and was soon to boast a membership of 450.

Wear coal shipments topped two millions tons. The total annual figure of 2,003,038 tons of coal was up by 4083 on the previous year and was boosted by exports to Denmark and Holland showing significant increases.

In 1960, the bulldozers moved into Howick Street and soon the first of 282 new flats and maisonettes in this redevelopment area became occupied at a weekly rent of 29/8d. Following large scale slum clearance at Monkwearmouth, the appearance of the Barbary Coast was changing rapidly but Sunderland Corporation vowed to preserve some of the area's former character by retaining many of the street names such as Barclay Street and William Street. Here, a small child watches as the bulldozers reduce houses in his street to a pile of rubble.

The former north end of Sunderland Railway Station. W H Smith's bookstall was situated on the left of the photograph while further up there was the popular children's machine which was used to print names on to a tin plate.

Work began on a £551,099 extension to Sunderland Technical College on a 14 acre site in South Johnson Street. The extension was built to house the departments of civil, mechanical and electrical engineering and, when complete, it would increase the college's capacity to 1800 full time students.

The new gas works opened at a cost of £20 million. The opening of the works marked a centenary of gas production on the same site although gas had been produced elsewhere in Sunderland since 1824.

The annual tonnage of ships built on the Wear was the lowest since the gloom year of 1954. In all, twenty five ships were built with an aggregate tonnage of 209,643 tons. This represented a downturn of 4000 tons over the previous year. For the first time in thirty years, the Wear Dockyard made no launches while Short Brothers of Pallion made just one launch. Southwick Shipyard headed the league table for the first time in its history with seven launches followed by William Doxford & Sons with five.

Plans were unveiled to develop the central area of the town as a pedestrianised shopping precinct.

Sunderland Corporation's three day Flower Show at Seaburn drew an all time record attendance of 18,666.

Proposals were put forward in 1960 for a new Civic Centre which would provide accommodation for all Town Hall departments including those which were scattered around the town. The proposed development was earmarked for a sixteen acre site in the West Park/Mowbray Park area of town. However, shortly after the proposals were put forward, the Minister for Housing and Local Government ruled that five acres of the development from Mowbray Park could not be used as the open space near to the town centre was a valuable asset to Sunderland as a whole. The scene here, originally intended for redevelopment, still survives today.

The text on this advertisement from 1960 would provoke much laughter today but in more innocent times it was quite acceptable.

The London & Newcastle Tea Company will be fondly remembered by many Wearsiders.

The stereotyped 3 piece suite of the early sixties. Every home should have one and all for just £48/5/0.

Sunderland Echo & Shipping Gazette, Monday, September 11, 1961

Echo
SUNDERLAND

No. 27,990 (88th YEAR)   TWOPENCE HALFPENNY
MONDAY, SEPTEMBER 11, 1961

SIX O'CLOCK

1,000 MORE JOBS FOR WEARSIDE
Transistor Radios To Be Made In New Pallion Works

A NEW radio factory on the Pallion Trading Estate, Sunderland, will provide 1,000 extra jobs, probably within the next 12 months.

The Board of Trade is to build a factory of 100,000 square feet for Perdio Ltd., London, for the manufacture and assembly of transistor sets.

Initially, it will employ 700 women and 300 men, with a possibility of future extension to double that capacity.

Plans for the new factory are to be submitted immediately to Sunderland Town Council and building is to start in the next few weeks.

Radio manufacture is a new industry to Sunderland although Associated Electrical Industries produce television tubes and radio valves at their Pallion factories.

Until recently there was one radio set manufacturer in the North-East. Thorne Electrical Industries at Spennymoor, but this was closed last year during the recession in the radio trade and production was concentrated in the company's London factory.

It is hoped that Perdio will use components manufactured in the North-East. The chairman and managing director is Viscount Stirdale and the company's headquarters are in Bonhill Street, London.

Mr R. E. Vidal, Industrial Development Officer to Sunderland Corporation, today confirmed that Perdio Ltd. was to establish a branch factory at Pallion.

"This development is particularly welcome as a means of absorbing more future school-leavers, especially girls."

12 MORE BODIES ARE FOUND

THE Red Cross reported this afternoon that 12 more bodies had been recover d from the wreckage of the air liner which crashed into the mud of the River Shannon with the loss of all 83 aboard. Sixty four bodies were recovered yesterday.

At low tide this afternoon recovery workers were hoping to break through the hull and release more bodies.

Airport engineers were also considering ways to get the wreckage to land so that experts could examine it to find the cause of the disaster.

Two More

Russia carried out two more nuclear explosions in the atmosphere yesterday, one of them involving a megatonnance device bigger than anything exploded since she resumed testing ten days ago, the U.S. Atomic Energy Commission announced today.

'SEXUAL ESCAPADES' AMONG TEEN-AGERS WORRY N.E. DOCTOR

A HEALTH report published in Newcastle today hits out at the "sexual escapades" of teen-agers. Their decline in moral standards, claims Dr. W. V. MacFarlane is largely responsible for a rise in the number of people needing treatment. Dr MacFarlane, physician in charge of the treatment of venereal diseases in the city says in the annual report of the city's health services that there were 1,065 new patients in 12 months and teen-agers in the lower age groups were providing one of the biggest problems.

Dr MacFarlane says: "Teenagers of the lower age groups are causing a great deal of concern and their sexual immorality is noticeable among those where there is a lack of parental supervision due to both parents working.

"Quite a few come from the better class homes and their parents would be horrified if they but knew some of their daughters' sexual escapades. Ignorance spreads disease and since these girls know little, if anything about venereal diseases they should be told the facts about this social evil."

PARENTS' RESPONSIBILITY

There was a decline in sex morals he said, in another section of the community. About one-third of all women requiring treatment h a d acquired the disease from "unfaithful husbands. "Now obvious explanation for the unsavoury conduct is forthcoming but this social problem —all too obvious in Newcastle over the past two years—demands urgent consideration"

Commenting on his report Dr MacFarlane, who is Medical Director of the Department of Venereology at Newcastle General Hospital, said today: "This is a problem which requires education of the parents as well as the children. Our interviews at the clinic **Continued in Page 3**

250,000 Flee Full Fury Of Hurricane

HOWLING 90 m.p.h. gales and tides nine feet above normal lashed the coastline of Texas and Louisiana today as Hurricane Carla, one of the biggest ever recorded in the U.S., moved in from the Gulf of Mexico.

The storms a portent of worse to come, flooded towns and smashed piers, boats, and beach houses. One squall killed a four-week-old baby and injured about 50 people in Kaplan, Louisiana.

TOWNS DESERTED

Towns along the 200-mile stretch of coastline expected to be hit by the hurricane were today almost deserted.

In a fantastic exodus over 250,000 people have fled to safer ground inland, leaving their homes barricaded in face of the approaching fury.

In hundreds of emergency shelters inland — churches, schools, and other buildings staffed by Red Cross workers — the evacuees listened on radios to hear what was happening in their home towns.

135 m.p.h. WINDS

Carla, with 135 m.p.h. winds raging at its 50-mile-wide centre, was about 110 miles out to sea and advancing remorselessly towards the coast at the rate of ten miles an hour.

Carla was expected to be the most intense hurricane to hit Texas this century.

Weather experts predicting the hurricane's course are being helped by photographs relayed from space by America's satellite Tiros III. Tides 12 and 15 feet above normal are predicted along the Texas and Louisiana seaboard when Carla hits the coast—enough to put large parts of many towns under water.

DANCER KILLED

DANCER Peter Keeme — known professionally as Pierre—was killed in a road accident today on the main Lowestoft-London Road. His wife, Cynthia — known as Desiree—was taken to hospital.

They were internationally famous and have appeared at theatres and cabarets in nearly all Continental capitals. They had been in a summer show at Lowestoft. It will go on as usual tonight.

The car is believed to have turned over several times. It stopped on its roof in the road.

His "Shocking" Writing

THE writing of Mr Edmund Tucker, headmaster of High Wycombe Royal Grammar School, was described by Amersham (Bucks) Magistrates today as "simply shocking."

Mr Tucker had written to the court pleading guilty to two motoring offences. The chairman, Mr E. C. Johnson, after reading the letter out with many pauses, commented: "For the headmaster of a grammar school, his handwriting is simply shocking; there are some words I just cannot read."

Mr Tucker, said to have driven for 40 years with a clean record, was fined £5 for parking within the limits of a pedestrian crossing and £3 for causing an obstruction.

IN SECRET HIDE-OUT

CONSTANCE LEVER
The Durham "riot girl"—home to a peaceful holiday. See story below.

Constance Gets Away From It

TWENTY - YEAR - OLD Durham student, Constance Lever, home from the United States where she was charged with inciting a race riot, relaxed in a secret hide-out "somewhere in England" with her parents today—away from the glare of the world's headlines for the first time since she upset the authorities in Monroe. North Carolina, 14 days ago.

No member of the Lever family was available for comment today but a friend told the Echo: "They have had a trying time and need a rest."

"NO QUESTIONS"

Constance, who was given a suspended sentence, was met by her father, Mr Walter Lever, a Durham University lecturer of Crossgate Peth, Durham, when she arrived back by air.

Miss Lever, who is studying at the London School of Economics, spent a quarter of an hour in an airport office talking to her father.

She later told reporters that she did not want to answer questions, adding: "With my father, I have prepared a statement and that is all I shall say."

She read: "I am pleased to be back in England and I am looking forward to being with my parents again. Newspapers have been calling me 'riot girl.' I've never been in a riot before and hope never to be in one again.

"UGLY EXPERIENCE"

"I did nothing to provoke it. It was an ugly experience. My companions and the people out of town and the people in the town especially the people in the town were among the finest I have met. I am proud to be associated with them. We all were fighting for the cause of equal rights for people of all races.

PARIS DOCTOR TO FIGHT FOR LIFE OF NORTH-EAST BOY

DR Maurice Gautrelet, Paris specialist in "Queen Bee Jelly" treatment, said today he would treat Tommy Harris eight-year-old boy from Middlesbrough who is dangerously ill with leukaemia.

He said he had received a telephone call from Middlesbrough and would see the boy on Wednesday. Tommy is due to fly to Paris with his father and go to Dr Gautrelet's clinic.

Tommy, of Orpington Road, Middlesbrough, is in hospital dangerously ill with leukaemia. Doctors have told his parents that he has only two weeks to live, but they are hoping he can be saved by Dr Gautrelet, who created a first record of this month.

"Of course I will see Tommy," said Dr Gautrelet, "I will do everything possible to save him."

"Queen Bee Jelly" is a substance exuded by worker bees which virtually controls the reproductive cycle in the hive.

Girl, Youth Found Dead

THE bodies of a girl and a youth were found today in a water filled dyke near Denton Isolation Hospital. Gravesend. Both are believed to have died from strangulation.

The body of the girl who was found first was unclothed and articles of her clothing were scattered nearby.

Police continued their search of the dyke. Information on a man who was interviewed at Snow Hill police station, London, had told them.

It was then that the body of a youth, a few years older than the girl, was found.

5,385 Jobs

He added that the new factory at Jackson the Tailor at Hendon was likely to engage a substantial number of women and girls in the near future and by the time the Perdio factory was built many more jobs would be available.

In his annual report, issued last week, Mr Vidal stated that the excess of school leavers over retirements in Sunderland in the next five years is expected to be 7,500. "There is therefore still need for more industry," he said.

Since Sunderland was classified as an area entitled to special assistance under the Local Employment Act projects which have been announced will provide employment for 5,385 men and women.

Hepworths and Grandage are constructing a works at Southwick which will employ 1,000 on the production of pistons and piston rings by the end of next year; Jackson the Tailor will shortly open their Hendon Road factory to provide jobs for 1,000; and James A. Jobling and Company have in hand a £2 million expansion programme which will increase their employment capacity by 1,200.

Other developments by Steels Engineering Products. David Brown Industries. and Ericssons Telephones Ltd., will provide work for another 1,185 people.

14 DIED

The death toll in the Monza motor race disaster rose to 14 today with the death of two more Italian spectators one of them a boy aged 14 who died in hospital said today. G men racing driver Wolfgang von Trips and 13 spectators were killed when von Trips' Ferrari plunged into the crowd at the Italian Grand Prix.

This Sunderland Echo headline greeted Wearsiders on 11th September 1961 as one thousand new jobs were announced for Sunderland.

IT WAS IN 1961 ....

Britain began negotiations to join the Common Market

South Africa left The Commonwealth

Ex Nazi officer Adolf Eichmann was executed for his war crimes

Off Course Betting was legalised and the country's first betting shops were opened

Mini cabs first appeared on Britain's streets

The Pill became available in the UK for the first time

The first Mothercare shop was opened

Britain's first self service petrol station was opened

The Avengers made its TV debut

Soviet Russia erected the Berlin Wall

Popular radio programme Children's Hour ended

The Tristen Da Cunha earthquake occurred

The first female Traffic Warden took to the streets of Britain

Yuri Gagarin became the first man in space

Tottenham Hotspur became the first soccer team in the 20th Century to win the FA Cup and League double

The first Bob Dylan LP was released

Go To Work On An Egg was the advertising slogan of the year

ABC's Thank Your Lucky Stars was launched by the ITV network

Are You Sure by The Allisons was the UK entry in the Eurovision Song Contest. It was voted into second position

West Side Story won Best Picture category in Academy Awards

Stirling Moss won BBC Sports Personality Of The Year

The one millionth Morris Minor rolled off the production line

In Sunderland in 1961...

One of the town's biggest employers, Associated Electrical Industries, announced that they were to start production of the new 19 inch and 23 inch square cornered television tubes. The news meant that the company's 'B' factory was employing 750 people in the manufacture of tubes while the 'A' factory employed 1500 people producing valves. As a result, the Sunderland site produced 30 per cent of all television components used in Britain.

Sunderland Town Council paid £78,000 for 1042 square yards of land in Union Street which was required as part of the town centre redevelopment project. The land was formerly owned by Sunderland Equitable Industrial Society.

Two of the town's best loved cinema's closed their doors for the last time. The Regent Cinema in Grangetown closed, following the Town Council's agreement to vary the covenant in the ground deed to allow the property to function as a supermarket. At that time, The Regent was one of the most modern cinemas in Sunderland being one of four built during the boom years of the late thirties. Some weeks later, the 900 seater Roker Cinema played to its final audience with a presentation of Walt Disney's 'Darby O'Gill & The Little People' on 8th April. The cinema first opened in 1914 and its closure made it Sunderland's seventh cinema closure in four years. The Town Council was considering a development application for a petrol station to be built on the site.

High Street West in 1961 when the north end of the railway station was still in use.

Wearmouth Bridge on a wet autumn night in 1961. A rear entrance double deck Guy bus of Sunderland Corporation heads for Telford Road as it is overtaken by a Bedford truck.

Plans were announced for work to start in 1962 on the rebuilding of the town's bomb scarred central station. It was intended that the new building would be one of a 'graceful, modern design' incorporating a cafeteria, waiting rooms, booking office and enquiries office grouped around a central concourse.

Wearside's unemployment dropped from 5.3 per cent to 4.0 per cent over the past twelve months. The number of people registered as being unemployed was 4064 which was the lowest figure since 1958. It was hoped that the figure would show further decreases as more jobs became available in the construction, shipbuilding, ship repair, transport and furniture industries.

The Council's plans to incorporate Boldon Urban District into the county borough received a setback with the announcement that the Local Government Boundaries Commission wanted the district included in its Tyneside Special Review Area. The Commission made it clear that it was to ask the Minister of Housing & Local Government to extend the Tyneside Special Review Area to include the whole of Boldon district as well as certain parts of Washington Urban District.

Two of the largest shipbuilding and engineering companies in Britain merged following fruitful negotiations between William Doxford & Sons and the Sunderland Shipbuilding Drydocks & Engineering Company.

A £35,000 scheme was put forward to demolish Havelock Towers in Hylton Road and build a new community centre and office block on the site. Havelock Towers had been used to house boys placed under the care of Sunderland Corporation until the closure of the building in March 1956.

Sunderland Corporation announced that all post war housing estates were to become smoke controlled zones, following proposals agreed at a meeting of the Health Committee. In all, 16,000 properties including a small number of privately owned houses were affected in an area covered by Hylton Castle, Hylton Red House, Town End Farm, Springwell, Thorney Close, Farringdon, Pennywell, Nookside, The Broadway and Hill View.

7,000 of the town's telephone subscribers were told that they would soon be able to dial direct to such places as Leeds, Aberdeen, Bristol and London thanks to a £50,000 investment programme by the Post Office. Time was bought in 2d units which bought twelve seconds of time for a long distance call at the full rate while it cost the same to buy twelve minutes of time for a local call at the cheap rate. Sunderland's 2,500 other subscribers on the Bishopwearmouth exchange were told that the direct dialling service would not be available to them until 1965.

Sunderland Corporation said it hoped that the building of the new town centre would start in early 1962 at a cost of £2.5 million and that the work would be completed within four to five years. Final plans together with compulsory purchase orders for properties in the 25 acre site were submitted at the March 1961 meeting of the Town Council. The plans to build a shopping precinct bordered by Union Street, Crowtree Road, High Street West and Blandford Street were subsequently approved as was the proposal for a one way traffic system around the square in an anticlockwise direction with stopping points on all sides.

The Busiris was launched from the Wear in 1961 and at the time was the river's biggest ever launch. The 38,000 ton turbine driven tanker was built for the Moss Hutchinson line of Liverpool and was the first launch from Joseph L Thompson's new 760 ft. berth which was situated between the North Sands and Manor Quay. The new berth was the biggest on the River Wear at that time and was capable of accommodating ships up to 65,000 tons.

In 1961, Sunderland Corporation proposed the demolition of 'three of the town's biggest eyesores." Work involved the transfer of the Reading Rooms in Fawcett Street to the new Central Library, large scale redevelopment of the area around Roker Blockyard and reconstruction of the Central Station area. This latter project involved demolition of the clock tower and other buildings at the north end of the railway station to make way for the building of new shops. The doomed railway station buildings are seen here on a site which is today occupied by the Littlewoods store.

Shipbuilding orders worth £2 million announced by Austin & Pickersgill and William Doxford & Sons meant that 18 orders had been received on the Wear during 1961 with a combined value of £22 million. The latest Doxford order was for a 14,500 ton vessel for West Hartlepool Steam Navigation Company while the Austin & Pickersgill order was for a 26,000 ton ore carrier for West Wales Steamship Company of Newport. This latter order encouraged the Southwick yard to consider extending one of its berths to accommodate large tonnage classes of ship.

Sunderland Education Authority finalised details for the purchase of Derwent Hill residential centre in Portinscale, Keswick and hoped that the centre would be operational by the summer of 1962. Derwent Hill, standing in 28 acres of land and overlooking Lake Derwentwater, was purchased for use as a base for Sunderland residents, predominantly school and college students, who were involved in outdoor educational activities.

Residents in the Sheepfolds area greeted the news of the intended demolition of their homes. Sunderland Corporation had made a compulsory purchase order for 144 houses as part of the slum clearance programme for the area which was designated an industrial redevelopment area. The 300 or so residents were to be re-housed in modern council homes.

Sunderland Shipbuilders made a drive for more Norwegian orders by setting up a 'shop window' in Oslo. During the first six months of 1961, four bulk carriers were launched on the Wear for Scandinavian owners and their aggregate tonnage of 78,000 tons was double the entire Sunderland output to Norway during 1959/1960. The Norwegian export initiative involved Sunderland Shipbuilders supporting a North East England Exhibition during early 1962 as well as playing host to a Norwegian Week which included a visit of the Bergen Festival to Sunderland Civic Theatre.

One of the town's biggest post war slum clearance projects took place in the Dame Dorothy Street area. The Minister of Housing for Local Government approved plans for Sunderland Corporation to serve compulsory purchase orders on 612 properties which had been earmarked for demolition. The project affected the lives of 3,597 people of which 847 were children and 230 were people living alone. Two of the properties each housed eleven people and there were also four families of ten, six families of nine and sixteen families of eight housed within the area.

The premises of Luxdon Laundry in Wycliffe Road were gutted by fire on 20th November. Damage was estimated at £100,000 and at the height of the fire, water was being poured on to the building at a rate of one thousand gallons per minute. The blaze was brought under control in ninety minutes by the sixty firemen and thirteen fire engines which attended the scene.

Sunderland AFC enjoyed a mini cup run in 1961 when, as a second division club, they beat first division Arsenal at Roker Park followed by a victory at Liverpool. The quarter final produced a home tie against first division leaders Tottenham Hotspur and a crowd of 61,326 saw the lads force a creditable 1-1 draw with the side who eventually went on to win the League and Cup double. The lads lost the replay at White Hart Lane. This photograph caught the crowds on camera as they made their way home following the drawn match at Roker Park.

Villette Road in 1961.

Nimble is the way she feels!

Up in the air! Full of bounce! That's the way you are on Nimble, the light, delicious bread. *Because* it's lighter. Lighter than ordinary bread. Tastes lighter. Feels lighter. And it satisfies you. Try it now. Choose brown, white, standard-sliced or thicker-sliced. All delicious. Live the Nimble way yourself and be the nimblest girl in town!

Eat **Nimble** – be nimble

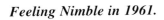

Feeling Nimble in 1961.

IT'S A
KEY MATCH
TOMORROW!

GET A COPY
OF THE

Football Echo
EDITION

AND READ ALL ABOUT
SUNDERLAND'S FORTUNES
AGAINST MIDDLESBROUGH

ALSO FULL POOLS RESULTS,
REPORTS AND RACING RETURNS

*A 'must' for all Sunderland AFC fans
then and now ... The Football Echo.*

The Minister of Housing & Local Government decided that land in Mowbray Park could not be used for the building of Sunderland's new Civic Centre. Scores of objections and petitions signed by hundreds of residents had been received at the Town Hall objecting to the council's proposals to use up 5.75 acres of Mowbray Park as part of the 15.61 acres development site and the Minister accepted the view that the open space near to the town centre was a valuable asset to Sunderland as a whole and should not be lost.

A false alarm occurred at Roker when the crew of a dredger working in the harbour entrance reported than an object resembling a sea mine had been brought up in one of the dredgers' buckets. Crowds of holidaymakers were cleared from Roker beaches and piers until the all-clear was given.

The engineering works of David Brown Industries moved to Sunderland from Huddersfield as the company's machinery was installed at the former Pallion works of Bristol Siddeley Engines Ltd.

The extensions to the town's central library were completed and resulted in a three fold capacity increase in book space in the building.

Sunderland AFC paid £45,000 for the signature of Middlesbrough's England International footballer Brian Clough.

Sunderland's Almshouses closed in July 1961 and with them another chapter in the town's history. A convoy of furniture vans moved off from Bishopwearmouth Green as eight elderly ladies locked the doors of the 240 years old Bowes Almshouses for the last time. They then set off for their new homes on the Town End Farm Estate. The Almshouses were later demolished as part of Sunderland Corporation's redevelopment plans for the area.

Sunderland Echo & Shipping Gazette, Monday, February 5, 1962.

Echo
SUNDERLAND

No. 28,114 (89th YEAR)   TWOPENCE HALFPENNY
MONDAY, FEBRUARY 5, 1962

SIX O'CLOCK

STRIKERS DRIVE AWAY WORK

Wear Loses A Valuable Contract To Holland

A DETAILED survey of the effects of the strike on Wearside and other parts of County Durham is in Page 6.

EMPLOYERS ACCUSED OF THREATS

AS 2,000 striking shipyard and engineering workers on Tyneside joined a pay protest which halted Newcastle's traffic today a union leader, Mr Len Edmondson, district secretary of the Amalgamated Engineering Union, alleged that employers in the area had threatened apprentices in a "series of private interviews."

Many of the workers who attended a meeting in St James's Hall shouted their support as Mr Edmondson, standing in the boxing ring, said: "If there are any reprisals against anyone tomorrow we will remember that a blow against one section or person is a blow against the whole of our members. We will feel entitled to retaliate accordingly."

"DOWNRIGHT LIE"

Mr Edmondson said: "Many employers have been attempting to intimidate apprentices by calling them into offices to interview them individually and warning them of the consequences if they came out on strike. They have been told that their terms of employment did not allow them to take part.

"This is a downright lie, he declared. "The apprentices are not taking part to support the adults. They are in this claim to better their own conditions. We must not let the employers touch the boys.

"If an employer wishes to make any complaint about an apprentice being out he should come to the trade union who called him out. I can't imagine a more cowardly or despicable act that to intimidate youngsters for responding to a trade union of which they are members."

DISAPPOINTED

Men in about 90 shipyards and engineering works on the Tyne and at Blyth responded to the strike call. Pickets were out in several places but there were no incidents.

Continued in Page 6

FRUIT DRINKS —COUNTY ANALYST HITS OUT

MANY parents buy fruit drinks for their children in the belief that they have a very much greater fruit content than is the case, Mr Joseph Markland, the Durham County analyst, declared today.

"The so-called whole orange drinks which contain the minimum two per cent fruit are not morally worthy of the name fruit drink," he states in his quarterly report to Durham County Council's Local Government Committee issued today.

Mr Markland says it is a pity that the Ministry of Food, while adopting new minimum standards for fruit drinks has not accepted recommendations that the fruit content of soft drinks should be declared.

ACTION DEPLORED

The new minimum standards for undiluted drinks was two per cent and ten per cent for those for consumption after dilution, but the Food Standards Committee would have recommended a higher standard if it had known its proviso requiring the declaration of fruit content was not going to be accepted.

The Local Government Committee deplored the action of the Minister in failing to adopt the recommendation that the fruit content of soft drinks should be made compulsory.

The committee has asked the County Councils' Association to take up the matter with the Minister and also a further recommendation that compulsory date-stamping of all pre-packed foods should be introduced.

Date stamping of all pre-packed food would help shopkeepers to sell their goods in rotation and would also enable customers to know if they were buying old stock.

ANOTHER SET OF QUADS

A WICK woman gave birth to quads, two boys and two girls, in hospital at Inverness, today. She is Mrs Alexander Jeppy, whose husband is a railway patrolman, and their family is now doubled as they already have four children, Robert (6), Alexander (5), Ian (4), and Mary (2).

Relations at Wick say the mother and babies are fine.

The last Scottish quads were born in Glasgow in 1959. In England, Mrs Phoebe Meacham (33), gave birth to quads — two boys and two girls — at a hospital in Essex on January 2 this year.

Strikers on the march. Instead of going to work these men marched through Newcastle to protest about their pay.

NOT ONE MAN AT WORK...

UNION leaders throughout Britain this afternoon said that today's national one-day token strike by three million engineers and shipyard workers was nearly 100 per cent successful.

The strike called by the 39-union Confederation of Shipbuilding and Engineering Unions over a pay and hours dispute, is the biggest stoppage since 1953 when the unions called for similar action in a pay dispute.

The strikers have staged protest marches in many industrial centres and at one meeting, in East London, Mr Ted Hill, the Boilermakers' secretary, said he was satisfied that there was not one man working in the shipyards of Britain.

A BLESSING IN DISGUISE . . .

Stoppage Eases London's Jams

LONDON'S big beat-the-jams one-way traffic experiment worked well on many roads in the rush hour, according to the motoring organizations.

But there were bad spots here and there, according to the Royal Automobile Club, which at the peak time said the results were "a bit like the curate's egg." The Automobile Association, which operated a spotter plane, said North London main roads became solid with traffic, while south of the Thames it ebbed and flowed, with holdings clearing themselves quickly.

50,000 FEWER

Patrols radioed "everything normal — no hold-ups."

Fifty thousand fewer passengers travelled by London's Underground in the rush hour although full services operated as a result of the cancellation of a repetition of last Monday's tube strike, which led to chaos on the roads.

London Transport attributed the ten per cent drop in tube passengers to many people having taken the day off after working at the week-end, and to the engineers' one-day strike which considerably reduced traffic in the factory belt areas.

Buses carried fewer passengers than usual and bus

inspectors reported fewer cars on the roads. Delays at some special road diversions meant some buses running up to an hour late.

Mr Ernest Marples, Minister of Transport, did not carry out his plan to cycle to his office today to see how the emergency arrangements worked. Hearing that things would be relatively normal he went by car.

> This notice outside the Sunderland shipyard of Joseph L. Thompson and Sons Ltd. invited anyone to come to work if they wished. Many Wearside works erected similar notices in response to a request by employers' organizations to keep yard and factory gates open—just in case. —S.E.

TODAY'S one-day token strike by Sunderland shipyard men has lost the Wear a valuable ship-repairing contract which would have lasted a fortnight and provided jobs for an extra 50 men.

Arrangements had been made for the Norwegian tanker Butanga (10,009 tons) to go into dry dock at Sunderland today, but when the owners learned of the one-day token strike by the Confederation of Shipbuilding and Engineering Unions they refused to allow the ship to come to the Wear.

The fortnight's ban on overtime by Wear shipyard-men also influenced the owners' decision to divert the Butanga to Rotterdam for repairs.

T. W. Greenwell and Company, of Sunderland South Docks, who were to have carried out the work, confirmed today that it had lost the contract but would make no comment.

The Butanga was in collision in the Thames on Wednesday with the Vacuum Pioneer, which is going to the Tyne for repairs. Both ships were badly damaged but in the case of the Butanga, she has a charter to meet and must be back in service in two weeks.

To Holland

When Greenwell's were unable to give this undertaking the contract went to a Dutch ship-repairer who offered to have the Butanga ready for service within a fortnight.

Thirty thousand Sunderland shipyard and engineering workers joined the one-day national token strike in support of a claim for more pay and a shorter working week. It is estimated that it cost the two industries in the town at least £50,000 in lost production and a similar amount was forfeited in wages by the strikers.

The Confederation of Shipbuilding and Engineering Unions called out its three million members after the employers rejected an application for a £1 a week rise and a reduction in the working week from 42 to 40 hours.

At most factories, works and shipyards, the men regarded the stoppage as "an extended week-end."

The Wear District Committee of the Confederation reported today that the strike was 100 per cent successful throughout the town. "Everything has gone according to plan and only maintenance men have reported for work in cases where special dispensations have been given," said Mr Herbert Wilkinson, secretary of the district committee.

BABIES DIE IN FIRE

THREE young Jamaican children died when fire swept through their bedroom in a Birmingham lodging house today. Brenda Rogers (5), Euston Rogers (4), and Joyce Rogers (2), were sleeping in a first-floor bedroom in the house while their mother, Linda Rogers (26), was out.

Another occupant of the house discovered the fire, but the room was already blazing too fiercely to be able to save the children.

The other people in the house got out safely, but two of them, Whitfield and Gwendoline Cox, had hospital treatment for cuts received as they escaped through a downstairs window.

WOMAN KILLED

A woman died and four men were rescued by turntable ladder in a fire in the top floor of residential flats in Welbeck Street, London, today.

The men, uninjured, were brought down from the fourth floor. The woman's body was found in a front room on the third floor.

The dead woman was Miss Amy Russell, aged about 50.

A one day strike by Sunderland shipyard workers on 5th February 1962 lost the River Wear a valuable ship repair contract which would have lasted for two weeks and created fifty jobs.

IT WAS IN 1962 ....

The first weather forecast was given in centigrade and fahrenheit

The last London smog occurred. It accounted for 28 deaths, brought traffic to a standstill and was London's worst smog for ten years

The communication satellite Telstar was launched, linking Britain and America

Television programme University Challenge was first shown

Dance craze The Twist first hit Britain

The Cuban Missile crisis was the year's main news story as America and Russia stood on the brink of nuclear war

Marilyn Monroe committed suicide

Nelson Mandela was jailed for five years for planning a National Strike in South Africa

Brazil retained soccer's World Cup

The Sunday Times published the first Sunday newspaper magazine supplement

Ring-A-Ding Girl by Ronnie Carrol was the UK entry in the Eurovision Song Contest. It was voted into second place

Lawrence Of Arabia won Best Picture category in the Academy Awards

Television satire show That Was The Week That Was — affectionately known as TW3 — was first transmitted by the BBC

Anita Lonsborough won BBC Sports Personality Of The Year

Love Me Do was released as the first single by The Beatles

The world's first Hovercraft service began with a trip across the River Dee. The service linked Rhyl in North Wales with Wallasey in Cheshire

Dennis Law became the first £100,000 footballer when he moved from Turin to Manchester United

The first James Bond film, Dr No, was released

Steptoe and Son made its television debut

Private Eye was first published

In Sunderland in 1962...

Sunderland Rural District Council expressed strong opposition to proposals to annex the existing Sunderland borough with Sunderland rural areas, including The Bents in Whitburn, saying that it regarded itself as a closely knit community with a different identity to that of the Sunderland borough.

Sunderland Corporation borrowed a massive £1,639,660 to finance redevelopment projects in the town. The figure included £500,000 to build 160 skyscraper flats and 16 maisonettes in Coronation Street.

Shipyard orders continued to come thick and fast during the second half of the year. Prestigious contracts included two placed with the Pallion yard of Short Brothers for a motor cargo vessel and a bulk carrier. The former was built for the Thomasson Shipping Company of Newcastle and was the first vessel to fully utilise the extensive modernisation scheme carried out at Short Brothers' yard. Meanwhile, Bartram & Sons announced that they had won an order to build the Wear's first ever car ferry. The order, to build the hull of a 3,000 ton car ferry, was sub-contracted to Bartrams by the German shipyard of Bremar Vulkan. Bartrams' success in landing the order was heralded as a great achievement for the British Shipbuilding industry. The ferry was designed to carry 650 passengers and 100 cars on the service between Copenhagen and the Danish island of Barnholm.

Sunderland Corporation Planning Committee approved plans for a £1,100,000 development of 600 houses at Carley Hill Farm.

River reflections at night. The Wear on a cold night in January 1962.

Robson's Flour Mills, once a prominent landmark in Chester Road became another part of Sunderland's history in November 1962 when demolition workers set fire to hundreds of wooden blocks beneath the foundations of the 50,000 brick tower. The building stood firm for an hour and then, as cracks appeared in the wall, the tower shuddered and collapsed into a heap of rubble. The Bishopwearmouth Flour Mills had been acquired by the Spillers Group in the 1930's and remained in their control until closure in 1959 when the company transferred its flour manufacturing activities to other sites. The land in Chester Road was purchased by Sunderland Corporation for expansion of Sunderland Technical College.

The first shipyard order of the year was announced by Austin & Pickersgill after they had secured the contract for a £1 million 20,000 ton bulk carrier. At the time it was the largest ever vessel to be ordered from the Southwick yard although later that year, the company won contracts for two 28,000 ton ore carriers. Other outstanding successes for Wearside shipyards during the first half of the year included orders for two 8,000 ton Blue Star liners and a 10,600 ton French cargo liner for Bartram & Sons as well as a 15,000 ton cargo carrier for William Doxford & Sons.

Craig Douglas and Bobby Thompson starred in Mother Goose at Sunderland Civic Theatre where panto goers paid 7s 6d for a seat in the Circle. Other blockbusting productions at the theatre in 1962 included the stage version of television quiz show Double Your Money with Hughie Green and Doctor In The House starring the cast of television show Emergency Ward 10.

New floodlights were installed at Roker Park which were among the most powerful lights at any football ground in the country. The new floodlights consisted of four towers, each 145 feet high and fitted with 48 lamps. They replaced the original lights which dated from 1952 at a time when Sunderland were one of the few football clubs to benefit from floodlighting at their ground.

One of the town's longest standing buildings was demolished. Pottery Buildings was built in 1868 as a bible depot by Edward Backhouse, member of a well known Quaker family. During its long history, the building also served as a welfare centre where teas were provided to foreign seamen and working men. The clock tower of the building was damaged during the second world war and there was little hope of ever restoring the East End landmark when it became structurally unsound in later years.

A fire at the works of British Ropes in July caused an estimated £100,000 worth of damage as thousands of tons of sisal were destroyed at the Roker Avenue site.

Uproar broke out following the decision of Sunderland Corporation Transport Department to withdraw the Circle bus service. At the time, the Circle was considered sacred by the residents of Hylton Road and Chester Road and within days of the service being scrapped, a petition calling for the restoration of the Circle was signed by 7,219 people. The bus service was eventually restored.

ERNIE, the equipment responsible for picking the numbers of Premium Bond prizewinners, operated from the town during a Premium Bond Investment Week.

The El Cubana coffee club opened in Toward Road.

Premises in Crowtree Road were among the first to be demolished once the redevelopment of the central area of town got underway during the early sixties. This photograph was taken in mid 1962 when two way traffic was still operational; a bus of the Sunderland District Omnibus Company heading east as it passes a Ford Classic. Although the newer properties in this photograph still survive today, the shops east of Moores store were demolished soon after the photograph was taken.

Brian Clough in action during the 1961/1962 season at Roker Park on a day when the lads beat Plymouth Argyle 5-0 in front of a crowd of 30,023. Cloughie scored a hat trick that day with the other two goals coming from Hooper. The team was: Wakeham/Irwin/Ashurst/Anderson/Rooks/McNab/Herd/McPheat/Hooper/Clough/ Overfield.

The new Binns store on the west side of Fawcett Street in 1962. It was in this year that a subway was constructed to link the stores on the west and east sides of the street at a cost of £15,000. At the time it was the only subway of its type in North East England.

The Gaumont cinema on the corner of Fawcett Street and High Street West shortly before closure. Note the tram lines from Sunderland's former tramway system which closed in 1954.

The century old engineering works of George Clark at South Docks closed when the lease on the premises expired. The works had been the home of steam reciprocating engines until 1956 when the collier Arundel became the final vessel to be fitted with that type of engine. From 1956 until 1962, the works were employed in the construction of low powered Clark-Sulzer engines suitable for coasters and colliers. A reduction in British coastal fleets resulted in a declining market for these engines and by 1962 the number of employees at the works had dropped from a late fifties peak of 750 to just 270. The works were demolished soon after closure, to become another chapter in Wearside's industrial history.

Durham County Council voiced strong objections to Sunderland Corporation's plans to build tower blocks of flats at Gilley Law, claiming that the proposed housing site was part of an area allocated on the Sunderland Development Plan for a public open space described as 'a most attractive area, well suited for use as an open space in this heavily populated region of County Durham.' Durham County Council added that, in their opinion, the tower blocks would dominate the area and an urban environment would be created by the towers and their associated roads and social facilities.

Sunderland Corporation were given permission by the Ministry of Housing & Local Government to borrow £46,750 to acquire and convert the former RAF station at Usworth into an aerodrome. It was claimed that the facility would greatly benefit industrialists visiting Wearside.

An incredible range of transistor radios from Palmers for listening to Jimmy Saville's TTDC and other Fab 208 programmes.

Two strong motoring names from the sixties were Standard and Triumph.

The switch from 405 to 625 lines was a revolutionary development in television history — and all for just 10/- per week.

Bargains galore at Binns on New Years Day in 1962.

SIX O'CLOCK

Sunderland Echo & Shipping Gazette

Echo
SUNDERLAND

No. 28,497 (90th YEAR)   THREEPENCE

THURSDAY, MAY 2, 1963

DUKE TO VISIT SUNDERLAND
Boat Trip On Wear Planned For July Tour

CAR WORKERS STRIKE OVER MAN'S SACKING
3,000 Idle And Production Halted

ALL car production was halted and 3,000 workers were idle at Morris Motors, Oxford, today because of an unofficial strike—the second in a week—over the dismissal of one man. Trouble at the factory began when Mr David Howes, a paint rubber who had been with the company for eleven years, was dismissed for alleged poor workmanship and misconduct.

His Royal "Double"

Film star Charlton Heston (above) will be the star in two premieres attended by the Duke of Edinburgh in London this month.

His Royal "double," believed to be the first in the history of the cinema, stems from a change of plan brought about by the illness of Burt Lancaster.

The Duke was to have seen the Italian film, "The Leopard," in which Burt Lancaster stars, at the Carlton, Haymarket, on May 27 in aid of the National Playing Fields Association and the Jewish National Fund. As usual a 20th Century Fox spokesman said today that the English dubbing had been delayed by the star's illness.

Now the Duke will see "Diamond Head," starring Mr Heston. The other premiere is at the Dominion Cinema on Monday when the film is "55 Days at Peking."

Palace Shelters?

In the Commons on Tuesday Mr W. W. Hamilton (Soc., West Fife) is to ask the Minister of Public Buildings and Works: "What provision for deep shelters is being made from public funds at the Royal palaces for protection in the event of nuclear attack?"

Other workers in the paint-shop came out on strike, but later returned to work so that talks could begin with the management. A works conference was held but trouble flared again yesterday when the men complained they were dissatisfied with the talks.

Last night, 310 paintshop men were on strike and another 1,800 were idle on the night shift.

Today, 374 paintshop men continued the strike, making nearly 3,000 others idle and paralysing production at the factory, which manufactures the Morris and M.G. 1100s, the Morris Minor, Morris Mini Minor, Morris Oxford Wolseley 1660 and 6110, Riley 472, and M.G. Magnette.

AT STANDSTILL

A B.M.C. spokesman in Birmingham said: "All vehicle production at the factory is at a standstill."

"This action of the strikers is against the advice of the district officials of the union who had instructed their members to remain at work. It is a contravention of the national agreement between the unions and engineering employers for the avoidance of disputes."

The spokesman added that the next stage after the works conference was a local conference. This had already been arranged, but could not now be held until there was a full return to normal working.

FORMER "MRS DALE" DIES IN HOSPITAL

MISS ELLIS POWELL, for 16 years Mrs Dale in the B.B.C.'s "Mrs Dale's Diary" until replaced by Jessie Matthews early this year, died today in a London hospital.

A spokesman at the National Temperance Hospital, London, said today that she was admitted yesterday afternoon through the emergency bed service and died early today.

Miss Powell became something of a national figure as Mrs Dale. She lived in a flat in New Cavendish Street, Marylebone, London.

Her marriage to actor Ralph Trueman was dissolved last June. They had been married 34 years.

Immediately the news of her dismissal was announced hundreds of listeners wrote to the B.B.C. in protest.

"Stop Reviling De Gaulle"
—WEAR M.P.

MR PAUL WILLIAMS, Conservative M.P. for Sunderland South, said in London today that Britain must stop reviling President de Gaulle and respect him for doing for France what many other European countries would like done for them.

He told the annual meeting of the Primrose League, that he has galvanized the French and produced a sense of national purpose we should well admire rather than criticize.

"We should pay tribute to General de Gaulle for reminding us that it was an island race and as a sovereign independent state that we climbed out of the rut of mediocrity and became a great power."

Mr Williams said that Britain hovered on the brink between greatness and obscurity, between grandeur and subjugation.

"The Aldermaston marchers shuffle and think with their feet, the pacifists preach, and T.W.T.W.T.W. destroys. A generation is adrift without a sense of purpose."

He said he was delighted the door for Britain's entry into the Common Market was now shut. Britain's needs were threefold.

To forget Brussels and no longer carry on the rancour, criticism, and pettiness arising from it and recognize the door was closed; to reject the idea of any further movement towards taking part in a European federation, and to return with renewed vigour to a Commonwealth-first policy.

Mr Williams also called for a Commonwealth space communications programme.

"It is not enough to latch on to the American programme. The Commonwealth needs a system of its own based on the pattern of Commonwealth trade, based on sterling and not on the dollar."

"GOVT. VISITORS HAVE NOT HELPED N.E."

ALTHOUGH a stream of Government Ministers had visited the North-East in the past 12 months, no real help for the area had been provided, Ald. Nicholas Garrow, Chairman of Northumberland County Council, said today.

He said that 12 months ago he had expressed the hope that the Council would get more Government help for schemes it was carrying out to provide for jobs.

He added: "We have had a stream of Ministers visiting us during the past year, but today there is no guarantee of any help.

"Meanwhile, unemployment gets worse in our county and in some parts we have no less than 11 per cent unemployed. This is tragic and cannot be allowed to continue."

"Greatest Man . . ."

FOLLOWING the announcement by Sir Winston Churchill that he is not to contest the next General Election in his constituency, the Woodford Conservative agent, Col. Hugh Barber-Wheeler, said today: "I am very sorry I shall no longer be connected with the greatest man in the world." He added that they had no prospective candidate in view.

Among leader comment in today's newspapers is one suggestion that Sir Winston should be made Britain's first honorary M.P.—as member for the Cinque Ports.

At his Hyde Park Gate home today, Sir Winston was said to be very fit after his night out at the Royal Academy banquet in London last night. As usual Sir Winston had his breakfast in bed reading the newspapers.

July Tour

THE Duke of Edinburgh will go for a 15-minute trip up the River Wear when he pays an official visit to Sunderland on July 26 to tour two shipyards and a glassworks which are contributing to the export drive.

The Duke is due to arrive in the town at 9.45 a.m. and will go straight to the North Sands shipyard of Joseph L. Thompson and Sons, where he will spend about an hour.

At the Manor Quay he will board a R.W.C. motor-launch to go upriver to Pallion, disembarking at William Doxford and Sons.

After half-an-hour in the shipyard, he will make his third —and final— call at the Wear Glass Works of James A. Jobling and Company for a quick tour of the factory. Then lunch will follow at the company's new £50,000 social hall at South Hylton. It will be about three o'clock in the afternoon when the Duke leaves the town.

His Request

The final arrangements for the Royal visit have to be decided at Buckingham Palace, but it is understood that it is the Duke's own request that he should make the trip upriver by boat. This will give sightseers on Wearmouth and Alexandra Bridges a chance to see him from an unusual vantage point.

The Duke is making the visit as part of National Productivity Year, with which he is so closely identified. The decision to make a five-hour tour of Wearside actually stems from an invitation from Jobling's to the Duke to see the developments carried out by the company.

That invitation was sent over a year ago but the Duke has waited a suitable opportunity to include visits to two shipyards. The decision to go to the North Sands yard has obviously been influenced by the fact that Thompson's are building an 80,000-ton tanker for Norwegian owners, the biggest ship under construction on the North-East Coast.

To Open Hall?

During his hour's visit, he will be able to see the mammoth tanker at close quarters before embarking at Doxford's. On the way up the river in a boat which will hold only ten people, places of interest will be pointed out.

When he steps ashore at Pallion, the Duke will go on a whirlwind tour of the shipyard, lasting about 30 minutes, before leaving by car for the Wear Glassworks. The exact details of his visit to the glassworks have yet to be arranged, but the directors will be his hosts at lunch.

It is possible—but not certain —that the Duke may open the new South Hylton social hall, which was completed in October last year for the company's 2,500

(Continued in Page 10)

Prince Philip Sees The "Imp"

THE Duke of Edinburgh, guest of honour at the formal opening ceremony at Linwood, Renfrewshire, today, of the new £23,500,000 Rootes Group factory, spent ten minutes inspecting one of the group's long-awaited Hillman "baby" cars, full details of which are to be announced tomorrow.

After standing back a few seconds to look at the lines of the bright red Hillman Imp, the Duke carried out a detailed examination from the engine compartment at the rear to the luggage compartment at the front.

He asked Lord Rootes, chairman of the Rootes Group: "Did you borrow anything from previous Rootes efforts?" Lord Rootes replied: "No. From the engineering point of view, it is completely new."

The Duke was told that the Imp was the first Rootes car to have independent all-round suspension, and that the aluminium engine could be changed by one man in one hour—half an hour to take it out, half an hour to put the new one in.

Today's visit began when the Duke, piloting himself in a Heron of the Queen's Flight, reached Renfrew Airport 20 minutes ahead of time. He had spent the night as a guest of Lord Rootes at Glenalmond Estate, Perthshire. Lord Rootes had travelled ahead to welcome him when he arrived.

On the way to the factory, at which the Imp will be produced, schoolchildren cheered the Duke as he passed. Several hundred people were at the factory gates to greet the Duke.

EXPANSION PLANNED

EVEN before full production has been reached at the new £23,500,000 Rootes car plant at Linwood, plans are already being made for a vast extension.

Demand for the Hillman Imp, with its rear-mounted aluminium engine, is expected to exceed the target production of 3,000 cars a week by the end of this year. Company officials predict an expansion which will more than double output.

The plant employs 1,700 workers at present, and the number will rise to 5,000 when target production is reached in seven months.

HAVE YOU SEEN THE NEW BROIDERPACKS!

They're complete embroidery packs! In a single glistening cylinder there's all you need to work a beautiful tablecloth, cushion cover, or traycloth, and many, many other articles. Every BROIDERPACK contains traced fabric, chart, needle and threads. And there are over 40 designs — the latest from leading makers. See BROIDERPACKS for yourself on the new *Display Stand* in our *Needlework Department!*

BINNS
SUNDERLAND

BINNS LIMITED SUNDERLAND TELEPHONE 6611

'Warships Seen Where Vessel Sank'

THE Japanese Broadcasting Corporation (N.H.K.) has reported that two unidentified warships—apparently cruisers—were seen today in the area where a Chinese cargo-ship sank mysteriously yesterday.

The crew of 59, picked up by a Japanese patrol boat and now on their way to Shanghai, claimed that the ship, the 9,482-ton Yue Jin, was sunk by three torpedoes, but Japanese officials had no confirmation.

"SEEN BY REPORTERS"

The Japanese Maritime Safety Board said neither the Japanese self-defence force nor the U.S. Armed Forces had any warships in the area at the time.

N.H.K. said in a television news broadcast that the two warships were seen by its reporters in a light plane. It showed pictures of warships which it said its reporters had seen.

The Yue Jin went down off South Korea while on its way from Tsingtao, China, to Moji, Japan, with a cargo of maize and other goods.

Headline story from The Sunderland Echo dated 2nd May 1963 concerned the visit of Duke Of Edinburgh to Sunderland on 26th July of that year.

IT WAS IN 1963 ....

The Great Train Robbery took place at Cheddington in Buckinghamshire as a gang held up and robbed the GPO mail train of well in excess of £1 million

President Kennedy was shot and killed in Dallas, Texas by Lee Harvey Oswald on November 22

Lee Harvey Oswald was shot and killed by Jack Ruby five days later

The Profumo Scandal rocked British politics. Central characters in the scandal included Doctor Stephen Ward and call girls Christine Keeler and Mandy Rice-Davies

Harold Wilson became leader of the Labour Party

The Beeching Report was first published recommending the closure of over 2000 railway stations and one quarter of Britain's railway network

Valentina Tereshkova became the first woman in space

First TV screening of TV cult programme Dr Who was made

The most severe winter for sixteen years gripped Britain

Sir Alex Douglas Home succeeded Harold Macmillan as Conservative Prime Minister

France rejected Britain's application to join EEC

Say Wonderful Things by Ronnie Carroll was the UK entry in the Eurovision Song Contest. It was voted into second position

Tom Jones won Best Picture category in Academy Awards

From Me To You gave The Beatles their first number one record

Cassius Clay beat British heavyweight champion Henry Cooper

Dorothy Hyman won BBC Sports Personality Of The Year

American Express credit card was launched in Britain but was only available to people earning at least £2000 per year

First rotary lawnmowers went on sale

Boutique became a new word in the English language as Carnaby Street in London established itself as a trendy fashion spot

George Best played his first game for Manchester United

TV pop programme Ready Steady Go was first broadcast by ITV. The show became a Friday night institution and used the opening words "The Weekend Starts Here"

In Sunderland in 1963...

One of Sunderland's oldest department stores, J. A. Kennedy Ltd., closed its doors in High Street West for the last time. The company had traded from the same site since 1885 and many Wearsiders regarded the closure of the store as a great loss to the town. The company announced that it would continue to trade from its smaller premises in Blandford Street which had opened in 1959.

The so called 'Little Ice Age' arrived as some of the heaviest snow falls since 1947 hit the town. Council workmen worked flat out to keep the roads open as emergency supplies of salt and grit became depleted as soon as they arrived. A gang of workmen were drafted into Roker Park to clear the pitch to enable the first leg of the League Cup semi final to go ahead on 12th. January. Unfortunately for Sunderland AFC, the snow clearing efforts were all in vain as the lads lost 3-1 to Aston Villa in front of a crowd of 33,237. Nick Sharkey scored Sunderland's goal while goalkeeper Jimmy Montgomery was carried off injured. Within six weeks, a staggering six million tons of snow had fallen in Sunderland.

The town topped the North East League for new housing. In post war years up to the end of 1962, 17,303 council houses had been built by Sunderland Corporation (132 more than in Newcastle) and 3671 private dwellings were built (1150 more than in Middlesbrough). In total, 20,974 new houses were built in Sunderland during this period compared with 19,327 in Newcastle. Sunderland also came out tops for demolition of older properties with 2745 edging ahead of the 2688 demolitions in Newcastle.

By 1963, the Cora Picture Palace had long since closed. The building was demolished in 1982.

On 27th March 1963 the Beeching Plan announced massive cuts of the region's railway facilities with the withdrawal of many passenger services. Large scale station closure in County Durham were also proposed as the Beeching Plan attempted to 'make the railways pay'. A major proposal was to withdraw all stopping passenger services between Sunderland and West Hartlepool and to scrap all passenger services on the Sunderland — Durham — Bishop Auckland and Sunderland — South Shields lines. Under the Beeching Plan, Cox Green station was earmarked for closure as 'a station which has been dying for years.' It was predicted by local people that the station's closure would completely isolate Cox Green as the riverside village was also without a bus service.

Washington Urban District Council offered to make available to Sunderland Corporation "a substantial number of houses" as well as 200 acres of land to meet Sunderland's overspill housing problems. Sunderland Corporation Housing Committee deferred a decision on the offer.

Plans to build a £200,000 bowling centre in Dykelands Road were called off after talks broke down with the Diamond Bowling Company of Canada. Meanwhile it was looking likely that plans for a £300,000 Bowling Centre in Newcastle Road would come to fruition. The proposals for the building included a ballroom, a bar grill, 32 bowling lanes and an underground car park.

Sunderland Town Council announced that it was to buy two pubs in Sunderland which would be subsequently demolished to accommodate re-development plans. The New Shades in Hendon Road was to be purchased for the sum of £5,925 and demolished as part of the Bramwell Street clearance project while the Shipwrights Arms in Dame Dorothy Street was to make way for the planned new road linking North Bridge Street with Harbour View at a compulsory purchase price of £3,413.

The Odeon was the principal venue for pop music concerts in the early sixties and the first touring package to visit in 1963 starred Helen Shapiro and also featured Danny Williams, Kenny Lynch, The Kestrels and The Beatles. There were two shows on 9th February, at 6.00pm and 8.30pm and ticket prices ranged from 3/- to 8/6d.

The 'Your Lucky Stars' touring package came to The Odeon on 27th February and starred no fewer than seven chart acts of the day in Joe Brown, The Tornados, Susan Maughan, Jess Conrad, Eden Kane, Rolf Harris and Shane Fenton.

Further pop concerts to be staged in Sunderland included a package starring John Leyton/Gene Vincent/Jet Harris & Tony Meehan at the Odeon on 30th March, Adam Faith at the Sunderland Empire for one week from 27th May, Eden Kane at Seaburn Hall on 1st June and Cliff Bennett & The Rebel Rousers at Seaburn Hall on 20th July.

21st March saw the official opening of Wetherells Club by television and recording star Ronnie Hilton. The club advertised itself as a Wining/Dining/Dancing/Gaming/Cabaret venue with two cocktail bars and boasted an extended drinks licence until 2.00am on a Friday, Saturday and Monday. Such late drinking hours were virtually unheard of outside London in those days and the owners said that it was their aim to make Wetherells into the finest nightspot in Northern England. Membership to the club cost one guinea.

The opening of Wetherells night club in March paved the way for a plethora of late night cabaret clubs in Sunderland. By 1963, a licence had been granted for a 'continental style' night club to be opened above the Westminster Bank in Fawcett Street. The club opened as La Strada.

The remains of the Almshouses are seen here in April 1963.

The Borgsten under floodlit construction in November 1963.

Two Sunderland girls holidaying in Majorca unexpectedly found themselves on the wrong side of the law after failing to observe a "no knees please" ruling when they went shopping in Palma wearing shorts which were less than knee length. They were arrested by Police and each fined the equivalent of 24 shillings while their hotelier was fined the equivalent of £3 for failing to inform his guests of the ruling on the island.

Doxford Engineering & Shipbuilding Group ordered a 63,000 ton tanker from one of its own companies — Joseph L Thompson & Sons. The order, which was worth £3 million, was for a tanker to be chartered by Shell Tankers and would guarantee work at the yard for four years. The order was secured with a loan from the Government Shipbuilding Credit Aid Scheme and was the ninth order to be placed with the Doxford Group since the scheme began, taking the total capacity to 338,000 tons. The value of these orders totalled £20 million which was approximately one third of the total budget allocated by the Government to ship owners.

Sunderland Corporation agreed to sell 18.71 acres of land at North Hylton Road to Air Products who hoped to start producing industrial gases at the site during early 1964 with the creation of 200 jobs.

Sunderland Education Committee took the first steps to abolish the 11 plus examination when they carried a motion that pupils from Red House and Town End Farm junior schools would transfer to Red House Comprehensive without a selection procedure, unless parents requested that their child take the examination.

In 1963, Seaburn Hall benefitted from a £4,500 refurbishment which it was hoped would attract more dancers in both summer and winter months. The improvements included the installation of a shell like glass fibre ceiling over the stage as well as new style decorating.

Cinema goers mourned the news that the Marina Cinema in Sea Road was to close its doors for the last time on 27th. July to make way for a supermarket. The date fell three days short of the cinema's 28th anniversary. The Marina had a reputation of being a family cinema, showing very few X rated films. It opened on 30th. July, 1935 with a showing of Things Are Looking Up and it was the first cinema in Sunderland to offer double seats without an arm in the middle — introduced for courting couples. Its closure made it the eighth cinema to close in Sunderland since mid 1961, leaving the town with just five survivors.

Following the launch of a Government Credit Aid Scheme for the shipping industry, Sunderland yards were among the major beneficiaries of the scheme which was aimed at stimulating demand for new tonnage. The Treasury announced that it would advance 80 per cent of the cost of building new vessels and this would be repayable over ten years at a fixed rate of 5 per cent interest. The first contract announced under the £30 million scheme was an order worth £1,100,000 for a 24,500 ton bulk carrier placed with Joseph L Thompson by R S Dagliesh of Newcastle. The order was announced on 24th. July and was quickly followed the following day by four further orders for the Wear. These orders created immediate work for four hundred unemployed shipyard workers at the yards of Austin & Pickersgill (where work commenced on a £1 million 20,750 ton bulk carrier for the Trader Navigation Company of London) and Wear Dockyard (where an order was secured for three non propelled vessels for the Admiralty.

Several thousand pounds worth of damage was caused when a fire broke out at the Wear Glass Works of James A. Jobling. The fire started in the old flint factory at the works and brought production to a standstill. Clouds of black smoke hung over Millfield and Deptford as twelve fire engines and six hundred men from Sunderland and Durham County fire brigades fought the blaze.

Sunderland's latest one way traffic system was introduced on 17th. April in West Wear Street when only south bound traffic was permitted to travel along the street.

Plans were announced for a new secondary school to be built at Pennywell. Plans revealed that the school would comprise five main teaching blocks each of which would be four stories high, an assembly hall, a sports hall, a swimming pool and a gymnasium. A workshop was also planned for a single storey block.

Sunderland Corporation Transport submitted an application to the Northern Area Traffic Commissioners to operate a bus service between Sunderland town centre and South Hylton. The application was opposed by W H Jolly whose buses had served a route between Hylton Road Schools and South Hylton since the twenties. A spokesman for Mr Jolly expressed the view that Sunderland Corporation were seeking to kill off the private bus service without having the honesty to buy it (Jolly had previously offered to sell the business to the Corporation). Not only did the private operator win the battle but he was granted a licence to extend his service fro. Kayll Road into the town centre and to introduce a weekday Works Service between Hylton and Pallion.

Stan Anderson leads out the Sunderland team at Roker Park at the start of the 1963/1964 promotion season.

Sunderland Echo & Shipping Gazette

Echo SUNDERLAND

No. 28,784 (91st YEAR)   THREEPENCE

SATURDAY, APRIL 4, 1964

SIX O'CLOCK

THREE ORDERS FOR THE WEAR?

Southwick Yard's Work Will Be Worth £4m.

THE Southwick shipyard of Austin and Pickersgill has reached an advanced stage of negotiations for three contracts for large bulk carriers worth about £4 million.

Two of the vessels are for the Chandris Group, which has had eight ships built on the Wear in the past ten years.

The latest vessels, 30,000-tonners, will be the largest ships to be built at Southwick, and it is intended to fit them with Sulzer machinery developing 12,000 horse-power.

As these bulk carriers are expected to be registered in Greece under Panamanian ownership, arrangements are being made to finance their construction under the Export Credits Guarantee Department. This would allow the owners to repay 80 per cent of the cost over ten years.

Negotiating

Delivery of the first bulk carrier is tentatively scheduled for June, 1965, and the Second in October next year.

Mr Kenneth Douglas, managing director of Austin and Pickersgill, said today: "Subject to satisfactory credit negotiations, these two orders will be placed at Southwick. Negotiations are at an advanced stage. We are also negotiating for another large bulk carrier for owners abroad. The three vessels will be worth about £4 million."

If these three orders are booked the tally of orders placed with Austin and Pickersgill in the past eight months will total ten ships valued at £15 million.

A Night Out Ends In Death

THREE electricians from Ashton - in - Makerfield, near Wigan (Lancs), were killed early today in a car crash on the London to Brighton road after a night out in London. They were staying in lodgings in Brighton during the week while they worked on an electrical contract at a poultry farm.

They were Frank Wilson (33), single; Alan Bailey (22), who was married last November, and Peter Ackers (19), son of the electrical contractor for whom they were working.

The driver of the car, which hit a lamp standard, Brianj Wynfield (22), a joiner, of St Helens (Lancs), was seriously injured and detained in the Sussex County Hospital.

Mr Bailey's wife, Doreen, is expecting a baby this summer, and was today under the care of her doctor suffering from shock.

QUEEN TAKES HER NEW BABY TO WINDSOR

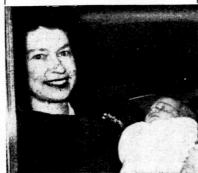

About 100 people standing in the rain outside Buckingham Palace waved to the Queen as she left today for Windsor Castle accompanied by Prince Andrew and her fourth child, who will be four weeks old on Tuesday. She is pictured here with the baby wrapped in a white shawl.

Today's drive was the first outing for the Queen's fourth child and also the first time the Queen has been out from the palace since the birth on March 10.

The Duke of Edinburgh, who had driven up from Windsor earlier in the morning, drove the Prince of Wales and Princess Anne in his own car. The Queen, hatless and wearing a red wool coat, was accompanied by Prince Andrew and Miss Mabel Anderson, the Royal "nannie."

The Queen and Prince Philip will be in residence at Windsor Castle until the beginning of May.

200 TRAPPED

Part of a girls' high school building collapsed today, trapping 200 students, in the heart of Madurai City, 350 miles from Madras. First reports said 40 people were killed and more than 100 injured.

Lawyers Study Ship Contract

Lawyers on both sides of the Atlantic examined "every full stop and comma" of the new freight contract form the U.S. Federal Maritime Commission is trying to force British shipping to accept, shippers and owners settled down to wait.

Back in his Liverpool office after talks yesterday with government and shipping officials, Mr Victor Springigs, Chairman of the North Atlantic West-Bound Freight Association, said today: "It is in the field of the legal people now."

Mr Springigs added: "We are getting opinions from our lawyers here and in Washington. I think it will be almost a fortnight before we get any real moves on the thing. They have a five-page foolscap document to go through and they have to watch every full stop and comma."

TO DISCUSS DEMANDS

He said his Association would meet in London on April 16. It was a routine meeting but would be the first opportunity for a round-table discussion of the American demands.

Mr R. G. Walton, Secretary of the North Atlantic Shippers' Association said: "We don't expect any further developments at the moment. It is being hammered out."

Mr Walton added: "Our own Government people, and the Ministry of Transport in particular, have been absolutely grand. They are taking it up extremely firmly with the American Government. We must wait and see what happens."

He said that unless a form of contract which was acceptable to both sides, were produced they would keep to their present contracts.

A Chamber of Shipping spokesman did not expect any early developments. "This thing is going to take some time," he said.

STRIKERS SAY "NO"

Eight hundred employees of William Doxford and Sons (Engineers) Ltd., Sunderland, today held a mass meeting at which they rejected the "peace proposals" of the management.

Doxford's yesterday suggested two ways in which the deadlock in the fortnight - old dispute could be broken by a resumption of work to allow talks to be held.

Coun. J. W. Loughran (pictured above), Sunderland area secretary of the A.E.U., told the Echo today: "I gave a complete report of what happened at the meeting with the management yesterday. The men unanimously rejected both proposals."

TRIO MISS TV

Top American folk-singing group, Peter, Paul and Mary, have had to cancel their "Sunday Night at the Palladium" TV appearance tomorrow because Paul (Paul Stookey) is ill with pleurisy.

ERNIE IMPROVES, ENTERS HOSPITAL

FORMER Sunderland and Newcastle United soccer star Ernie Taylor managed a smile for Melbourne reporters who visited him in his cabin in the Greek liner Ellinis today and said he felt "a lot better" after receiving blood transfusions yesterday.

A Royal Australian Air Force plane flew from South Australia to parachute blood plasma beside the ship after Taylor (38) was reported to be critically ill and losing blood from a perforated ulcer.

Taylor, looking pale but cheerful, paid tribute today to all who made the mercy flight possible. The Ellinis's master, Captain Zenios, had radioed the agents in Melbourne for help, and police and the R.A.A.F. co-operated to organize the air lift.

The ship's doctor, Dr Alexander Charitou, said Taylor's condition was much improved, but it had been decided to take him to Prince Henry's Hospital in Melbourne for a thorough examination. He might stay there three weeks. His wife and their children would stay at a hotel.

Taylor, who was to have arrived in Auckland, New Zealand, on April 15 to become player-coach to New Brighton Football Club in Christchurch, said today he did not know what effect his illness would have on the plans, but he was still looking forward to teaching youngsters the game.

Mrs Taylor told reporters her husband's illness had been a great shock as "he had never suffered anything like this before."

Mr and Mrs Taylor, who had lived at Hyde, Cheshire, since his retirement from football about 18 months ago, decided to move to New Zealand "to get a little sunshine," Mrs Taylor said.

They had been running a public house in recent months.

Coaster Sinks, Bodies Found

THE 282-ton German coaster Nordmark sank in the North Sea today and rescue ships picked up the bodies of three of her six crew. The Nordmark, which radioed an S O S early today, sank six miles west of the Borkum lightship, Norddeich coastal radio reported.

Ships searching the area off the Friesian Islands found two lifeboats amid floating wreckage, but no sign of the remainder of the Nordmark's crew. Helicopters joined the search.

The Nordmark, of Hamburg, was bound for Hull with a mixed cargo. It was her first voyage after a dockyard overhaul.

Later, radio reports said the rescue ships had abandoned the search for survivors.

SECOND SIAMESE TWIN DIES

JANE, the 3½lb. Siamese twin who survived a separation operation at Birmingham Children's Hospital last night died today, said a hospital spokesman. She lived nearly 12 hours after being separated from her sister, Susan, who died last night. They were joined at the abdomen.

The babies were born on Thursday in Hallam Hospital, West Bromwich, to a mother whose name was withheld at her own request.

The New Zealand - born flautist John Amadio (77), collapsed and died in Melbourne today while rehearsing with the Victorian Symphony Orchestra.

shop at Binns

HOME ENTERTAINMENT

72gns   71gns   72gns

EKCO 19in. TELEVISION model T418T fitted for 625 reception. Walnut veneered cabinet. 72 Gns. (Stand extra)

PYE 19in. MODEL 114 TELEVISON. Complete 625 set. In dark walnut finish.
71 Gns.

PHILIPS 19in. T.V. model 17TC155A. No extras to buy for 625 reception.
72 Gns. (Stand extra)

H.P. TERMS

All goods available on Hire Purchase Terms, or by Budget Account (Ask for booklet).

(Bottom left) FERGUSON TRANSISTOR model 3114. In simulated leather case. Suitable for playing in a car.   12 Gns.

EKCO TRANSISTOR model PT378. Handbag type transistor. In blue or red leathercloth.
Price 13½ Gns.

DYNATRON RECORD PLAYER model GR8A. This model is for the quality enthusiast and is fitted with the Garrant AT6 auto-unit. Large output amplifier.
Price 29 Gns.

29 Gns.

BINNS GAY TRAY CAFETERIA

After the match, visit Binns Gay Tray Cafeteria for tea or high tea. Open until 6.0 p.m.

BINNS LIMITED SUNDERLAND TELEPHONE 4411

Good news for the town's shipyard workers came with this announcement of a likely £4 million contract won by Austin & Pickersgill for the construction of three large bulk carriers.

IT WAS IN 1964 ....

BBC 2 was first transmitted

Ian Smith became first Prime Minister of Rhodesia

Topless dancers went on show for the first time in Britain

Pierre Point carried out final UK hanging

Donald Campbell broke the land and water speed records

The Forth Bridge was opened

English Bank Holidays were moved from the first to the last Monday in August

First edition of Top Of The Pops was broadcast from a disused church in Manchester

Harold Wilson's Labour Government was elected

Radio Caroline, anchored off the Essex coast at Felixstowe, became Britain's first pirate radio station to take to the air

Mary Whitehouse announced the launch of her Clean Up TV campaign

I Love The Little Things by Matt Monro was the UK entry in the Eurovision Song Contest. It was voted into second position

My Fair Lady won Best Picture category in the Academy Awards

Beatlemania hit USA and at one time The Beatles occupied the top five positions on the American singles chart

Cassius Clay became World Heavyweight Champion when he beat Sonny Liston

Brezhner replaced Khrushchev as Soviet Prime Minister

Mary Rand won BBC Sports Personality Of The Year

A pint of beer rose to 2s 1d and a packet of twenty cigarettes rose to 4s 10d in the budget

The first major tussle between the Mods and Rockers took place during Easter at Clacton and was followed by many confrontations between the two self styled groups including a seaside showdown at Margate on Whit Sunday of that year

The final edition of The Daily Herald hit the news stands on Sepetmber 14. The following day saw the launch of Britain's first National newspaper for 34 years when The Sun made its debut

Match Of The Day was televised for the first time

In Sunderland in 1964...

Durham Road Methodist Church closed for worship on 30th August. The 62-year old church, the head of the old Durham Road Wesleyan Methodist Circuit, was originally built to replace the Fawcett Street Wesleyan Methodist Church.

The former Boilermaker's hall, once a landmark in High Street West, was demolished in 1964 to make way for a block of shops and offices. It was used as a bank before passing to the Boilermakers Society who used it for about 20 years until the early 1930's. For many years it stood empty and prior to being demolished it was occupied by a tailoring company.

T.I. Tubes of Birmingham announced its intention to build a £1.5 million factory on a site between Usworth and Washington which would create 350 jobs.

Sunderland Education Authority caused an outrage when it revealed plans to revert to comprehensive education at Bede Grammar School.

Sunderland Corporation announced plans to spend a record amount of £6,151,804 on housing in 1964/1965. The largest single project involved the building of 889 flats at Gilley Law, many in sky scraper blocks at a total cost of £3,290,150. Other expenditure involved residential building work at Carley Hill. Downhill, Witherwack and Thristley Hall as well as slum clearance projects in the Dame Dorothy Street area (at a cost of £728,000), Hendon Road area (£746,500) and Hahnemann Street district (£315,000).

The bulldozers have been and gone as the Lawrence Street area of town awaits redevelopment.

This unusual view of demolition work at the south end of Sunderland's Railway Station was taken from a second floor room at the Town Hall.

It was announced in 1964 that Bainbridge Holme, parts of which dated back to the fifteenth century, was to be demolished to make way for a re-development comprising six detached houses. At that time, Bainbridge Holme was the oldest inhabited house in Sunderland. In the main the building was Georgian and it was reputed to contain a `Priest Hole' in which priests were said to have hidden during times of the oppression.

The last occupied cottage in Carley Place, Southwick awaits demolition. Many of the cottages in the once populous area were over 100 years old when they were demolished to make way for Sunderland Corporation's new housing project.

This changing face of Fulwell shows the framework of the former Marina Cinema being demolished to make way for a supermarket.

A rural scene two miles from Sunderland town centre which disappeared in 1964 was Witherwack Farm in Southwick which was demolished to accommodate a new housing estate.

The Church of the Venerable Bede was demolished in 1964 after being closed some years earlier. The closure followed a population shift from the Newcastle Road area.

A £6 million shipbuilding order was won by the Wear as Bartram & Sons announced a contract for three fully refrigerated cargo liners for the New Zealand Shipping Company Ltd. It was the Wear's largest new contract in nine months.

The underground tunnel mystery deepened on 9th July with the discovery of another tunnel — the third in recent weeks — on a building site at the corner of Church Street. Tunnel finding had become a popular pastime and speculation as to their origins was reaching fever pitch. Brickwork of the tunnels suggested that they had been built midway through the nineteenth century and one theory was that they were used to smuggle contraband goods ashore to public houses at Low Quay and Ettrick Quay. Some years earlier, sealed off tunnels had been found under churches and factories and in one find, a collection of coins had been recovered.

The giant Borgsten tanker was launched. At 85,600 tons, it was the biggest tanker ever built in Britain and the largest merchant ship launched since the Queen Elizabeth. It was built at a cost of £3.5 million for Fred Olsen & Company of Oslo. At the launch from the North Sands yard, Mr R. Cyril Thompson announced that recent expansions meant that the yard had room available for a second berth to take ships up to 100,000 tons.

Sunderland Corporation announced a "massive push" to rid the town of its council housing waiting list. This included the building of 12,000 houses by 1969. The plans were unveiled at a ceremony which had been called to announce the completion of the 14 storey high Dame Dorothy Street superstructure which itself was part of a £1.5 million redevelopment scheme. With plans already underway to build a 20 storey block of flats — 200 feet high — the skyline of Sunderland was set to change forever.

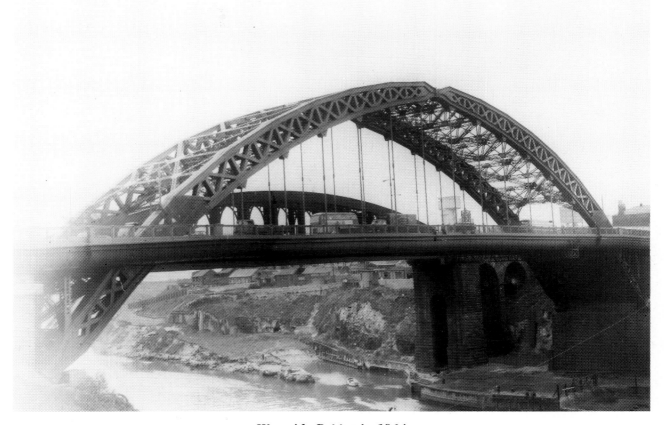

Wearside Bridge in 1964

Banish those washday blues with the incredible Hoover Spinarinse.

New! Terrific! Electric! Refrigerators from the NEEB.

Records to suit all tastes in 1964.

Near riots took place at Roker Park when Sunderland entertained Manchester United in an F.A. Cup sixth round replay. An estimated crowd of 100,000 travelled to the ground and while an estimated 70,000 people managed to get inside, only 46,727 actually paid. The others burst open the double gates at the ground and forced their way in. Two fans died, one hundred were treated at the Accident Hospital and Royal Infirmary and sixteen people were admitted with broken limbs. The fact that the match was not all-ticket contributed to the chaos, Sunderland AFC claiming that there was insufficient time to have tickets printed. The match ended in a 2-2 draw with Sunderland's goals coming from Sharkey and Setters (own goal).

The reconstruction of Athenaeum Street bridge was completed and British Railways announced plans to start rebuilding the south end of the railway station followed by the demolition of the north end.

The Football Echo was printed on pink newspaper for the first time in six years as Sunderland won promotion to Division One. The Football Echo has turned white (many people said with shock) when Sunderland were relegated for the first time in their history on 26th April 1958. The newspaper had been printed blue ever since, with the promise that it would revert to its traditional pink colour when the team were promoted to Division One or won the F.A. Cup. Goals from Herd and Crossan gave Sunderland a 2-1 home win against Charlton Athletic before a crowd of 50,827 to ensure promotion and the return of the pink Football Echo.

In January, a public enquiry investigated a proposed alteration to Sunderland Corporation's £2.5 million central area redevelopment plans which involved making High Street West into a pedestrianised thoroughfare with a brightly lit underpass, 265 feet wide, at the junction of High Street West and York Street.

The Pallion shipyard of Short Brothers announced its closure during 1964. Since the yard was founded in 1850, it had built 540 ships and during the Company's peak post war period it employed over one thousand men. The last ship to be built at the yard was the 20,750 ton bulk carrier Carlton which was completed in January of that year. The yard's closure was attributed to a lack of financial resources to extend its berths to build the bigger ships of the day.

T.W. Greenwell announced that the recent ship repair boom at its yard was likely to continue despite the uncertain prospects generally being felt in the industry. The high degree of British and continental competition was not damaging the company as keen bidding, prompt delivery and good workmanship were winning the day, it was claimed.

Charlie Hurley leads out Sunderland during the 1964/1965 season. This was Sunderland's first season back in the top flight after six seasons in the Second Division wilderness and a season which started with fifteen year old Derek Forster playing in goal in place of the injured Jimmy Montgomery. When this photo was taken, Monty was back in the side and is seen here following Len Ashurst onto the field.

N 1965 ....

alty was abolished

dvertisements for cigarettes were banned

'0 mph speed limit was introduced

Tax was introduced

hurchill died, aged 90. He had been a Member of th

ws was knighted

hy Kirby was UK entry ir
oming the sixth consecu

sic won Be t Picture

Jnilate   pe

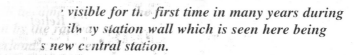

*This west side view   visible for the first time in many years during
1964. It had previo   by the railway station wall which is seen here being
demolished to make   s new central station.*

*The changing scene at Hendon in 1964 as houses, shops and pubs were demolished in the
Hendon Road/Lawrence Street area. Sunderland Corporation had accepted a tender of
£1,205,384 by a contract company to build 414 dwellings in this redevelopment area.*

In Sunderland in 1965...

The Empire Theatre enjoyed its most successful season under municipal ownership in 1964/1965. Audiences totalled 227,511 compared with 192,107 in 1963/1964. During 1960/1961, the first full season of corporation control, audiences totalled 120,813.

It was all change at Roker Park as Sunderland AFC ended manager George Hardwick's 168 day reign and promptly offered the job to Scotland's manager Ian McColl. Many fans felt that George Hardwick had been treated harshly, having taken 27 points from 26 games with the team well clear of relegation.

The Perdio Electronics factory announced its impending closure with the loss of 580 jobs. The Pallion factory which opened in November 1962 never reached full capacity and blamed its failure on cheap radio components being imported from the far east.

Five hundred new jobs were created when the British & International Addressing Company opened premises on a 5.5 acre site in Hendon Road. The Company who claimed to be the country's biggest direct mail organisation, said that there would be up to 1,000 additional part time jobs for 'at home' work for housewives.

Jim Baxter became Sunderland's most expensive signing when he left Rangers for a fee of £75,000.

The site of the former Gaiety Theatre in High Street East which was demolished in 1965. The scheduled redevelopment for the site was an eighteen storey tower block which would become the highest in Sunderland.

One of the first demolition scars to be inflicted upon Fawcett Street in modern times was in 1965. The form Gaumont Cinema site.

Sunderland Corporation Housing Committee released plans to build 600 houses, flats and bungalows at Witherwack Farm Estate. Meanwhile, the Watch Committee rejected plans to introduce parking meters in the town centre but gave the go ahead to traffic wardens taking to the streets to help, not impede, the motorist.

One hundred jobs were created when Olin Mathieson Mine Equipment Company of London relocated its factory site in Middlesex to Sunderland.
A further boost for Sunderland's unemployed came with the news that Ericssons Telephones in North Hylton Road were increasing their workforce at the factory by 800 to over 3,000 people. Output on the site had increased by 15 per cent in twelve months.

Sunderland Education Committee were asked to approve plans to amalgamate the two Bede Schools to one mixed Comprehensive School in time for the September 1967 intake of pupils.

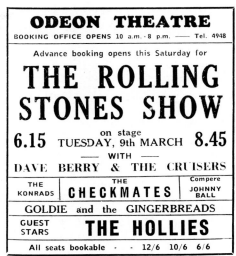
*The ultimate sixties pop show!
The Rolling Stones and The
Hollies on one bill in 1965.*

*Three of Sunderland's major
night spots in the sixties were
the Locarno, Wetherells and
La Strada.*

On 4th. January, the People's Republic of China ordered its first two ships from a British shipyard when it placed a £2.5 million contract with William Doxford & Sons. The order was for two 15,000 ton fast cargo liners and followed a visit of a five man shipbuilding mission to Peking in 1964.

Plans to build a multi-storey car park in Tavistock Place were announced. The car park, the first of its type in Sunderland, would have spaces for 500-600 cars and would cost £160,000 to construct.

British Rail announced that the South Docks Marshalling Yard would close in early March. The yard, which was opened in the nineteenth century to match the port's expanding trade, dated back to the time when the port was in its early days. By the early 1900s, increased traffic led to an extra seven acres of land being acquired from the Town Moor to expand the port's activities. By the early sixties, the volume of traffic began dropping and the news of closure came as no surprise. Forty men were made redundant as a result of the closure.

Formal objections to the changeover of Bede School to comprehensive education were submitted to the Permanent Under Secretary of State for the Department of Education and Science. Ojectors included the Sunderland Committee for Educational Freedom and the Old Bedans Association.

Following their success in landing a shipbuilding order for the People's Republic of China, the Doxford Group "cracked" the iron curtain by securing an order for two 14,800 ton cargo liners from Industrialexport of Bucharest. These would be the first Romanian ships to be built in Britain for thirty years. The Doxford Group placed the order — worth £2.75 million — with their James Laing & Sons Deptford Shipyard.

As over 30,000 workers with £1 million in their pockets left Sunderland's shipyards and factories for their annual holidays, the Sunderland Echo reported that thousands of Wearsiders were spending their money in search of the sun throughout Europe.

It was a boom time for the shipbuilding industry, thanks to the Government Aid Scheme. Further orders included a £1.5 million passenger ship for the Transoceanic Steamship Company of Karachi (for Bartrams) and a £8 million order for four 44,000 bulk carriers for a Norwegian operator (for Austin & Pickersgill). This latter order was the largest ever secured by the Southwick yard at that time but it was placed subject to the approval of the export credit guarantee department. This Government department acted as a guarantor for the cost of new ships and would only do so, after checking the credit worthiness of foreign ship owners.

Sunderland Town Council rejected a Health Committee recommendation that fluoride should be added to the town's water supply.

This aerial photograph of Sunderland was taken in 1965 with New Durham Road, The Green and Chester Road areas of town clearly identifiable.

These were the early boom years of overseas package holidays. According to one local travel agent, the most popular destinations were Spain and Yugoslavia.

One of the wildest Saturday nights/Sunday mornings in the town's history followed a 'friendly' at Roker Park between Sunderland and Celtic. The invasion of an estimated 6,000 Celtic fans brought a reign of terror to Sunderland as drunken louts went on the rampage. Fifty people with Scottish accents were treated at Sunderland Hospitals. The chairman of Sunderland's Watch Committee vowed that Glasgow soccer fans would never again be allowed into Sunderland.

Sunderland's 20,000th council house was completed. This was a post war house building record for any county borough of a similar size to Sunderland and an important landmark in the town's history.

Orders worth £500,000 were received by Newalls Insulation & Chemical Company for contract insulation work on power stations at various UK sites. Newalls was the largest British company engaged in land based insulation contracts and its Washington based company employed 1,500 people at that time.

Sir Basil Spence outlined his plans to Sunderland Town Council for the proposed new Civic Centre to be built at West Park. At a subsequent special meeting of Sunderland Town Council, the plans for the £3,333,500 project were approved. The chairman of the housing committee told members that the next step would be to apply to the Ministry of Housing & Local Government for a loan sanction to cover the scheme. It was hoped that work would start in Spring 1967.

Building of a new approach road to the north end of Alexandra Bridge started.

An unusual story published in the Sunderland Echo on 13th July concerned a 66 year old widower from Margaret Street whose house had been demolished and furniture destroyed while he was a patient at Sunderland General Hospital. Chairman of Sunderland Housing Committee commented, "The house was in a clearance area and the occupant would have been advised of that fact and requested to remove his furniture." Sunderland Town Council claimed that an eviction order had been issued and that the furniture had been removed lawfully or unlawfully by persons unknown. Sir Jack Cohen, speaking for Sunderland Town Council, was quoted as saying that he wished to make it clear that the council had never demolished a house without the owner being told first! Also, the council had never demolished a house while the furniture was still inside!!

A Modern Transport System For Sunderland was published by the town council. The study proposed a flat fare of 3d for journeys on the town's buses in or out of the town centre or 6d for a cross town journey. The system would use one man operated single deck buses with passengers using pre-purchased bus tokens to qualify for the low cost fares. The proposals were passed by the Transport Committee on 1st July. A similar system was already successfully operating in Copenhagen.

The offices and workshops of Sunderland Corporation Transport's Wheatsheaf Depot were extensively rebuilt during the mid sixties. This photograph dates from December 1965.

A bungalow at Hastings Hill from only £2,597 although garage is extra!

A real shocker from 1965.

In Sunderland in 1966...

Sunderland Corporation announced re-development plans for the Stoney Lane area of town as bulldozers moved in to demolish many of the older properties. A compulsory purchase order had seen served on a 12.76 acre area in December 1964 which involved 170 dwellings which were deemed to be unfit for human inhabitation. Some 230 families were affected by the decision which was an extremely controversial one at the time and one which caused much bitterness as the council was accused of needlessly breaking up an entire community. 75% of the properties were over 90 years old and reasons given for the demolition included rising damp, varying stages of disrepair, a lack of essential facilities (including internal water supplies and WCs) and overcrowding.

Sunderland Technical College and the College of Art were awarded Polytechnic status by the Secretary of State for Education & Science. Sunderland was one of 30 centres chosen nationally for the creation of Polytechnics.

On 15th October, the NCB made the shock announcement that Ryhope Colliery was to close by the end of the year. The colliery was the major employer of male labour in Ryhope and it was estimated that after some miners were found alternative employment at Wearmouth, Westoe and Boldon Collieries, some 300 men would be facing redundancy. News of Ryhope's closure was surprising in the light of recent expenditure totalling £100,000 on colliery equipment and current production levels of 800-900 tons of coal per week.

By October 1966, the bulldozers and the redevelopers had arrived in Newcastle Road.

The launch of the Mari Chandris in 1966.

The Top Rank Suite and The Locarno, two of Sunderland's luxury ballrooms, were granted publicans' licences in January. Both venues had previously obtained occasional licences and no trouble had occurred at any of the events.

World Cup fever hit Sunderland during the first few days of 1966 and, by 7th January, Sunderland AFC had banked over £8,000 in ticket sales for the Roker Park games. This represented ticket sales of approximately 3,000 of the 13,348 on sale at the ground with prices ranging from £1 10s to £8 16s. The three games staged at Roker Park were Chile v Italy (13th July), Italy v Russia (16th July) and Chile v Russia (20th July).

Sunderland's teenage girls found it difficult to buy a drink at many town centre hotels unless they were accompanied by a male escort. The Continental Hotel and Palatine Hotel both commented that their public bars were besieged by teenage girls at weekends and holiday periods and many of their regular customers were unhappy about the situation. It was reported that some of the girls were actually under 18 years old and that this was placing bar staff in a difficult situation.

Sunderland Corporation Transport Department announced that the ship from Sunderland's Coat of Arms would be imprinted upon the town's bus tokens which were due to come into use during September. The design was said to be characteristic of the town's activities and at the same time it would remind people of their Coat of Arms. The reverse side of the tokens would bear the lettering: SCT. 1 Journey.

CLUB LIFE ★ NEXT WEEK

One of the first Sunderland Echo advertisement features devoted to club life in the town.

The former North End of Sunderland Central Station in 1966. A pile of rubble stood where taxis once waited for passengers under the familiar old canopy. The adjoining Finlays did a roaring trade with the town's smokers. Littlewoods store now stands here.

Sunderland was chosen for the country's first five yearly census. Ten per cent of the town's population was selected to answer twenty questions about their jobs, families, professional qualifications, car ownership, means of transport to work etc. Previously, a census had been carried out on a ten year basis.

Work started on Sunderland's first multi-storey car park, in Tavistock Place. When completed, the car park would house 604 cars on nine split levels. Cost of the project was estimated at £179,832.

Contractors moved into the derelict site behind Union Street on 24th June to start work on creating a 20th century shopping complex on the ten acre site. Plans included provision for a three levelled area comprising two supermarkets, 74 shops, a department store, a hotel, 300 flats in a multi storey block, a bus station, a market hall and roof top parking for 250 cars.

Opposition to the decision of the Minister of Housing and Local Government to extend Sunderland's boundaries increased following the announcement that Herrington Parish Council planned to stage a protest meeting. They were followed in their action by other parish councils whose principle concerns were anticipated increases in rents and rates, education, housing policy (and the theoretical likelihood that people from council houses within the parish could be rehoused in any part of Sunderland and the fact that rural community spirit would become a thing of the past. Parish councils which joined the fight against the merger of Sunderland Rural District with Sunderland included Tunstall (who were "against the carve up of Sunderland Rural District"), Ford (who said that the proposals would "terminate village life as known") and Hylton (who were prepared "to resist the decision to merge their parish council with Sunderland").

A five week old dispute between Vaux Breweries and their employees became official on 27th January. The strikers walked out in sympathy with 80 draymen who had been sacked on New Years Day for working to rule following a dispute concerning the company's employment of non-union men. The strike was called off when support diminished.

September 1966 saw the introduction of the flat fare system on Sunderland Corporation's buses. It cost 4d cash or one token for a journey of any distance. Tokens cost 2/9d for ten. Many routes switched to Pay As You Enter with single deck buses replacing the older double deck vehicles. Bus No. 54 is seen here at Roker on first day duty.

The entire North East was spoilt for choice on the night life scene in 1966.

Liverpool House making the most of Easter 1966.

As Sunderland prepared for the World Cup Final games at Roker Park, it was announced that an all-day drinks licence extension to midnight had been granted to Seaburn Hall for the duration of World Cup fortnight — but only for overseas visitors to Sunderland. Seaburn Hall would be run as a club for the benefit of visiting supporters who, in their own countries, could purchase alcohol at all times of the day. Meanwhile, the town's transport department entered into the spirit of things when it announced its intention to display the flags of the three competing nations on the roofs of selected buses during the games. Predictably perhaps, local shopkeepers were apathetic towards contributing to the festivities commenting via Sunderland's Chamber of Trade that they would not decorate their premises without the Corporation first presenting suggestions and details of cost.

The Sunderland Echo reported that one Sunderland street was under siege. Houses in Chester Terrace had had their windows boarded up either to prevent them being broken or because they had been broken. For four days and nights, a missile thrower had been throwing lumps of concrete over the roof tops. The culprit had not been caught despite the presence of police patrols, tracker dogs, the fire brigade, rooftop searches and the use of searchlights. Even in daylight, with people standing on the street, the missiles continued to arrive. At the time, there was even talk of the supernatural being at work.

World Cup tickets being snapped up at Roker Park.
(Above)
A Sunderland Echo promotions feature for the World
Cup games at Roker Park in 1966. (Left)

Sunderland Corporation entered into the spirit of the World Cup games at Roker Park by
decking out a number of its buses with flags of the competing nations.

Sunderland Town Council was asked by the Planning Committee to refuse an application for a bingo stall in White's Market. The application involved a request for change of use of part of a fruit stall to a bingo stall which the Planning Committee considered to be inappropriate for an indoor market, siting congestion and disturbance as the main reasons for objection.

Sunderland's new one man operated buses took to the roads on 5th September. The single deck vehicles seated 47 passengers with 19 standing. A flat fare of 4d or 1 token was charged. Tokens cost 2s 9d for ten. At this time, the Ministry of Transport gave the go ahead for Sunderland Corporation to build a new municipal bus station adjacent to the shopping area development and to borrow £316,000 to finance the project.

As interest in the World Cup Finals reached fever pitch, hundreds of overseas football supporters surged through the streets of Sunderland waving flags, blowing horns, shaking rattles and singing football songs. Wearsiders looked on in bewilderment as Italian and Chilean supporters thronged Fawcett Street from one end to another shouting to their opposite numbers in their native tongue. The atmosphere was good natured as many fans told the Sunderland Echo that they were delighted to be in Sunderland and thought that the people were very nice. Meanwhile, Wetherells Club offered temporary employment to interpreters fluent in French, German, Italian, Spanish, Greek, Russian and Korean to encourage visitors to the region (Sunderland and Middlesbrough) to visit the club.

As for the games themselves, 27,199 fans attended Roker Park on 13th July for the opening game which saw Italy beat Chile 2-0. This was followed three days later by a 1-0 victory for Russia against Italy in front of a crowd of 27,793. In the concluding game at Roker, 16,027 fans saw Russia score a 2-1 win against Chile.

The Wear Winch & Foundry Company in Spelter Works Road announced that it was to close in October. Founded in 1907 with premises in Park Lane, the company later moved to a new site on the cliff tops at Hendon. In its heyday, the company produced winch castings, engine castings and deck castings for Wearside and Tyneside shipyards but with shipbuilders using less cast iron by the mid sixties, the works had ceased to be an economic proposition. The closure resulted in 41 redundancies.

Sunderland to have six day trading? That was the shock announcement made on 19th October. The introduction of Wednesday afternoon trading in Sunderland's main shopping streets would bring the town into line with Newcastle and other major urban areas. It was reported in the Sunderland Echo that Wednesday afternoon opening would meet the needs of women working in industry although shops would not be compelled to switch to six day trading.

BIA Direct Mail Ltd opened a £300,000 factory in Hendon Road to produce, address and distribute advertising material to millions of British households.

Shipments of coal from Sunderland fell by 201,406 tons during 1966. A significant feature of the fall was the large drop in overseas shipments which totalled just 85,014 tons compared with 200,104 in 1965. Total tonnage of shipments in 1966 was 1,928,999 tons.

Sunderland Echo & Shipping Gazette

Echo
SUNDERLAND

No. 29,636 (94th YEAR)   FOURPENCE
TUESDAY, JANUARY 3, 1967

SIX O'CLOCK

WASHINGTON: A "NEW WORLD"

"Showpiece Of North" Will House 80,000 In "18 Villages"

WHEN the long-awaited master plan for the Washington new town was made public today at a conference attended by Press and television representatives from all over the country and from the United States, Sir James Steel, chairman of the Development Corporation Board, said that the plan had been produced "right on target."

Sir James said the master plan had been produced after some 29 months from the time when the new town was first designated. The new town would comprise what he called "18 villages" and form a new world where people would live, work and play.

"Here will be a people dynamic, adventurous, and equipped with the skills required to exploit the new materials and manufacturing techniques of industry, eager to grasp the opportunities offered. Washington of the future will be a place where people will be proud to live and the showpiece of the North." he said.

Sir James added that when fully developed Washington would have approximately 765 acres of industrial land and by the end of the century there would be a population in the new town of 80,000.

It was hoped that the first families would move into new houses, at present under construction in the Welbank Road area of Washington, by the autumn of this year. Thirty per cent of the houses would be built in the new town would be for sale, ranging from £4,000 to £15,000.

The new town's 18 "villages" would each have their own particular "identity" and shopping facilities.

Rents

In answer to a question Sir James said that the rents of houses to be built by the Corporation would be between £3 15s and £5 per week. The Development Corporation was quite confident that there would be the people to occupy these houses.

Answering a further question, Sir James said that as the new town developed and when the plans for industry progressed Washington's "eyesore," the Washington F. pit heap, would disappear.

Mr. Stephen Holley, general manager of the Corporation, said that the administrative centre of the new town would be based near the Washington Village area where the Urban District Council offices were situated. "It will be connected with the shopping centre by a formal pedestrian mall which may have recreational facilities and amenity areas along its way."

"The administrative centre will contain the local authority offices, Crown Buildings, police station, and magistrates court and any larger-scale offices which are attracted to the town."

Answering further questions, Sir James said the three primary

Continued in Page 13

Ship Calls For Aid

THE 29,230-ton Liberian tanker Failaika, with 43 men on board was reported to be in distress about 600 miles east of New York today after losing some of her superstructure in heavy seas. A U.S. Coast Guard spokesman in New York said the tanker reported that her master had a broken left arm, but there were no other injuries.

The spokesman said the tanker later reported that she was proceeding under her own power but she still needed assistance.

FACING GUNS CHARGES

A GREEK Cypriot newsagent, Christos Costas (30), of Pratt Street, Camden Town, London, was accused at Bow Street, London, today of selling three revolvers to Harry Roberts, in connexion with firearms. He is charged with possessing a Luger, a Colt, and an Enfield without certificates, with selling these to Harry Roberts without the buyer producing a certificate, and of being in possession of a colt revolver and ammunition in a public place.

Det. Supt. Richard Chitty, who headed the investigation into the murders, in asking for a remand, said there was no objection to bail.

SEVEN MiGs SHOT DOWN NEAR HANOI

ALL seven Communist jet fighters shot down in the biggest air battle of the Vietnam war yesterday were MiG 21s, the most modern type the North Vietnamese Air Force has, a U.S. spokesman said in Saigon today.

More than 50 U.S. F-4C Phantom jets ranged over North Vietnam and brought down the Migs with air-to-air heat-seeking missiles. The battle was fought at supersonic speed about 20 miles north-east of Hanoi above the major North Vietnamese Mig base at Phuc Yen.

Air Force officials said that 14 flights of Phantoms, the most modern operational jet in American use in the war, were sent over North Vietnam with the sole purpose of seeking out Communist planes.

"We sent them up as a fighter sweep with the idea of engaging any MiGs that wanted to be engaged," General William W. Monyer, Commander of the U.S. Seventh Air Force, told a Press conference in Saigon today.

SOVIET-DESIGNED

He said that until yesterday it was estimated that the North Vietnamese had 15 to 20 of the modern Soviet-designed MiG 21's. Altogether the North is believed to have about 100 MiGs, mostly older-model MiG 17's.

The Phantoms were flying cover for Air Force F-105 Thunderchiefs attacking ground-to-air missile sites when the MiGs rose to challenge.

Since the air war started in August, 1964, American pilots claim to have shot down 34 MiGs, and lost 10 of their own planes to enemy fighters.

"HAPPIEST PART"

Air Force Colonel Robin Olds (44), whose wing shot down six of the North Vietnamese planes, said: "The happiest part of the day was that the Migs had chosen to tangle with us. That is what we had hoped for."

British Offer Rejected

NORTH Vietnam, in a denunciation of Britain's offer to arrange cease-fire talks on the Vietnamese war, said today it was a foul act running completely counter to the responsibility of a co-chairman of the 1954 Geneva conference on Vietnam.

An uncompromising commentary in the official Hanoi newspaper Nhan Dan, carried today by the North Vietnamese News Agency, declared: "It is the U.S. imperialist aggressor who have started the war in Vietnam. If this war is to be ended at all the U.S. must stop its aggression and withdraw its troops from Vietnam."

"END BOMBING"

It reaffirmed the four-point stand of the North Vietnamese Government for a settlement and the five-point statement of the South Vietnam National Front for Liberation on the Vietnam issue.

It also demanded that the United States end its bombing of North Vietnam and recognize the South Vietnam National Front for Liberation.

The paper said the British proposal was but a move to force the Vietnamese people to negotiate under pressure and accept the "insolent" U.S. terms.

"Such a foul act on the part of the British Government completely runs counter to the responsibility of Britain as a co-chairman of the 1954 Geneva conference on Vietnam."

"UNDER PRESSURE"

The Soviet Communist Party newspaper Pravda today attributed the British peace initiative to a delicate situation facing Mr Wilson's Government through pressure of public opinion. It said: "The British Government has found itself under exceedingly strong pressure from public opinion demanding its dissociation from the U.S. aggression in Vietnam.

"It must have been because of this and in an effort to find a way out of an extremely delicate situation that the British Government launched Brown's 'peace initiative'."

JERSEY MURDER APPEAL

AN appeal to the public to help solve the murder of attractive 20-year-old Finnish Girl, Miss Tuula Hook, found battered to death in a field in Jersey last Saturday, was made today by Chief Officer James Axon, head of Jersey Police.

Mr Axon said he was anxious to contact anyone who saw Miss Hook after she left her St Helier address in heavy rain on Friday evening, to catch a bus to go to a party. She never got to the party.

Just over 12 hours later, she was found by a local farmer just inside a meadow along a lonely lane near St Clements Parish Church, about three miles east of St Helier. It was estimated she had been dead about 12 hours.

"There is no motive for the murder of Miss Hook," said Mr Axon. "She had not been sexually attacked, and as far as I know nothing is missing from her handbag."

A simple map showing now building Washington New Town will strengthen the Tyneside - Wearside link.

Paintings: £1,000 Reward Offer

THE governors of Dulwich College, London, announced today that they are offering up to £1,000 reward in connexion with the theft from the college art gallery of eight paintings worth £1,500,000.

It will be paid for information leading to the recovery of all or any of the pictures.

Mr David Banwell, clerk to the governors, said: "We are not paying a ransom and are not interested in the people who stole the pictures." He added: "The money won't be paid until the police give us the all clear."

"ON THE TRAIL"

Following information obtained in the West End, police officers carried out investigations in Central and West London during the night, and believe they may be on the trail of the thief or thieves.

A gallery spokesman said last night that the gallery may be open to the public within a day or two, but stricter security arrangements were to be made. Security arrangements were enforced in Sheffield yesterday to guard the 35 Rembrandt etchings on loan from the city's Graves Art Gallery from the Victoria and Albert Museum.

BLAST AT PLANT

TWO men needed medical treatment after an explosion today at the Whitehaven (Cumberland) chemical plant of Marchon Products. Extensive damage was done to the plant. A lid blew off a reactor starting a fire which was quickly put out.

The plant operator, protected by a blast wall, was treated for shock, and a contractor's employee was taken to the West Cumberland hospital, Hensingham, with minor injuries.

The company said there would be a detailed inquiry.

LEFT £7,000

Detective Constable David Stanley Bertram Wombwell (25), of Eastfield Court, East Acton Lane, London, one of the three policemen shot dead in Shepherds Bush on August 12, left £7,609 (£7,529 net), it was announced today. Duty of £227 has been paid. Detective Wombwell left a widow and two children.

Sir James Steel (second left), Chairman of the Washington Development Corporation, pictured at today's Press conference with, left to right, Lord Llewelyn-Davies, consultant planner, Mr W. S. Holley Corporation General Manager; Mr Walter Bor, consultant planner, and Dr Dorman Christopherson, a member of the Corporation.   —S.E.

The long awaited master plan for the creation of Washington New Town was made public on 3rd January 1967.

IT WAS IN 1967 ....

The world's first heart transplant was performed by Dr Chris Barnard

Donald Campbell was killed on Lake Coniston in his speedboat Bluebird as he attempted to break the water speed record

The breathalyser test was introduced

BBC 2 was first broadcast in colour

Abortions were legalised

The QE2 was launched

The pound was devalued

BBC Radio was reorganised with the creation of Radios 1,2,3 and 4

Celtic became the first British football club to win the European Cup

Puppet On A String by Sandie Shaw won the Eurovision Song Contest for the UK

In The Heat Of The Night won Best Picture Category in Academy Awards

First TV screening of The Forsyte Saga and Dr Who were made

The first large scale arrival of the hippies occurred during the so-called Summer Of Love

The Beatles released the legendary Sgt Pepper album

The Torrey Canyon ran aground off the Cornish coast spilling 100,000 tons of oil into the sea

Henry Cooper won BBC Sports Personality Of The Year

The first North Sea gas was piped ashore at Easington by BP

The first bank cash dispenser was introduced in Britain

Brian Epstein died

News At Ten was first broadcast by ITN

Beanz Meanz Heinz advertising slogan was first used

Dance troupe Pan's People made their first appearance on TV pop programme Top Of The Pops

In Sunderland in 1967...

Lambton Staiths closed for good on 7th January. The Staiths first opened in 1812 to load shipments of coal from Hetton and Herrington collieries into the colliers trading between Sunderland and the South. The Staiths' heyday was undoubtedly during the late thirties when they handled as much as 45,000 tons of coal per week. The decline in shipments began in the late forties and by the time of closure, only 2,000 tons of coal per week was being loaded there. This business was transferred to South Docks Staiths in Sunderland.

During the 1966/1967 financial year, it was reported that Sunderland Corporation's buses operated at a loss of £206,000. Mr Norman Morton, manager of the undertaking, said that if the system had not reverted to the recently introduced one man operation, the deficit would have been £265,000. The Transport Committee were asked to consider either raising fares or raising the subsidy from the rates from 4d to 6d in the pound to offset the deficit.

Sunderland's first peace-time female corporation bus driver took to the road in February when Pat Entwhistle sat behind the wheel of a Fleetline bus on service 16, from Town to Grindon. She was followed later in the day by Joyce Beaumont on service 2, from Town to Farringdon.

The old and the new. The old Wheatsheaf offices with scaffolding in place prior to demolition. The replacement offices stand immediately behind. A Hillman Imp, Ford Consul and Morris Minor represent a bygone age of motoring.

Many of the town's drinkers mourned the passing of the Bridge End Vaults which bit the dust in 1967 to allow the building of the new inner ring road.

Although it is December 1967, there is very little festive cheer in Bridge Street as the end is nigh for these properties, including the Bridge End Vaults.

The Warwickshire prepares for launch in 1967.

Sunderland Corporation Seaside Development and Entertainments Committee considered yet another scheme to make Seaburn Hall justify its existence with a proposal to use the building as an indoor bowls centre with bar facilities during the winter months.

Washington Development Corporation disclosed that it was negotiating with the treasury for the re-location of the Royal Mint to Washington. Sir James Steel, chairman of the Development Corporation revealed that negotiations had been taking place since August 1966 but had been a closely guarded secret at the treasury's insistence. A site had been selected by the Royal Mint, details of building requirements were being discussed and the Development Corporation was leaving nothing undone in its efforts to influence the Royal Mint to move to Washington.

4th March was the final day for rail passengers to board or alight from trains at Monkwearmouth Station.

White's Market had all but vanished by 16th September with only the perimeter walls remaining. They too would soon disappear as the site was cleared to construct a new market hall and car park.

The results of a survey first published in the Sunderland Echo showed that the prospect of people in County Durham owning their home had risen since 1961. More houses than ever had hot water systems and baths while 33 per cent of the population were car owners. Sunderland had 55,130 dwellings which were occupied by 58,060 families, 19,220 houses were owner occupied and of the town's 34,440 families living in rented accommodation, 26,830 were council tenants.

19,629 fans turned up at Roker Park for Charlie Hurley's testimonial match against an international eleven which included such big names as Bonetti, McCreadie, Cooke, Osgood (Chelsea), Peters, Moore, Hurst (West Ham) and Hinton (Derby). Final score was 4-4.

Pioneering Sunderland Corporation Transport manager, Norman Morton, resigned following the announcement that the town's buses were continuing to operate at a loss, having carried 67,413,155 passengers which was 3,470,193 fewer than in the previous year. It was reported that in his letter of resignation, Mr Morton gave his reasons for resigning as being the council's alleged indifference to public transport and their desire to abandon the flat fare system. In an act of supreme pettiness, Mr Morton was asked to pay thirty shillings to the Borough Treasurer to cover the postage costs of his resignation statements which he had sent to all councillors explaining his reasons for resigning.

A fire engine attends a fire in High Street East on 26th October 1967.

Pann Lane in October 1967.

*The Moody Blues at Wetherwells in 1967 prior to
them achieving super stardom status.*

Wearside's two biggest co-operative societies, Sunderland and Ryhope & Silksworth, merged to give a combined membership of 47,000 and annual turnover of £3 million. Price cuts were promised as a result of the greater buying power of the merged societies.

Radio 270, the pirate radio station which entertained Wearsiders for much of 1966 and 1967 went off air at 11.59 p.m. on 14th August as it played out with the National Anthem. One minute later, the Marine Broadcasting (Offences) Act came into force with the power to jail or fine persons found guilty of illegal broadcasting. Radio 270 was based at Bridlington Bay, Scarborough and was one of only three pirate radio stations broadcasting when it was forced off air by Government legislation.

Solvent abuse was a problem even in the sixties. On 2nd November, a judge told Sunderland juvenile court that the habit of sniffing a well known substance was a form of drug taking which was prevalent on one of Sunderland's outlying estates. Two boys aged fourteen were accused of stealing the substance from a Sunderland shop. The judge warned of the effect of their habit to the eyes, brain and body.

On 26th November, the railway bridge which carried the main line from the South Docks over Hendon Road was demolished and, within hours, a new 200 ton replacement bridge was winched into position. The headroom of the new bridge was 16ft. 6in. compared with 14ft. 2in. of its predecessor. This was made possible by excavating the road underneath. It was Sunderland's first new railway bridge since the construction of Roker Baths Road Bridge in 1931.

A £50,000 link road scheme was proposed for the area across the old Gill Cemetery to link Silksworth Row and Paley Street.

Wednesday Specials at Blacketts who, in 1967, took the bold step of opening all day on a Wednesday.

Announcing Phosferine in Bitter Lemon flavour!

The Bachelors at Atkinson's record shop in 1967. Atkinson's were the town's principle record dealer with outlets at Athenaeum Street and White's Market. Here the Bachelors met fans at the Athenaeum Street shop where EP and LP sleeves were displayed around the walls. Remember 'Emitex'?

Sunderland Corporation prepared to do battle with the private bus companies in its efforts to bring cheap municipal transport to residents in the town's new territories. The corporation's Transport Committee approved an application to be submitted to the Traffic Commissioners to run express type services at peak periods to Ryhope, Herrington and Silksworth at a 6d flat fare.

So much for the swinging sixties! A Sunderland Corporation planner told a public enquiry that to allow prize bingo in a restaurant at Queens Parade, Seaburn would be the thin end of the wedge in establishing a 'Golden Mile' along the seafront and that a 'Golden Mile' was not the policy of the corporation. Opposing bingo at the Merry Go Round restaurant, Mr Snowball, on behalf of Vaux Breweries (owners of the near-by Seaburn Hotel) was quoted as saying, "People who are attracted to this type of amusement are usually, to put it bluntly, out for a bit of fun and people who want a bit of fun may be the type who will be tempted to commit vandalism."

The growth in unemployment among Wearside shipyard workers was discussed at a meeting of their union delegates with Mr Dan Smith, Chairman of the Northern Economic Planning Council. Speaking generally about unemployment in the region, Mr Smith's words of comfort were that the North East must stop moaning about unemployment and do everything possible to help itself.

Sunderland Echo & Shipping Gazette

Echo
SUNDERLAND

No. 29,979 (95th YEAR)   FIVEPENCE
SATURDAY, FEBRUARY 10, 1968

1968

SIX O'CLOCK
WEAR JOBLESS PROTEST MARCH
—But only 39 people go "on parade"

"PLEASED TO BE BACK"

Sunderland's new manager, Mr Alan Brown, pictured in happy mood at yesterday's Press conference at Roker Park immediately after his appointment. —S.E.

ONLY 39 people, some of them union officials, turned out in Sunderland today to follow Sunderland Trades Council banner in a protest march against unemployment in the town, which in January totalled 6,367.

The march, organized by the Trades Council, was the first of its type in Sunderland for many years.

The marchers, including one woman, gathered at West Park, Sunderland. Carrying the Trades Council's banner, which bears the slogan "Unity is Strength," and escorted by one policeman, they walked down Burdon Road and along Fawcett Street to the Town Hall, causing a slight traffic hold-up for a few minutes.

Throughout the journey some of the marchers shouted the slogans "Stop unemployment, Wilson must go" and "Wilson out. Socialism in."

Several more people joined the marchers at the Town Hall, and by the time everyone was settled in the Reception Room the numbers had grown to more than 100.

On arrival they were urged to buy the publications Keep Left and Workers' Fight. Mr J. G. Gray, who contested municipal elections last May as an English Nationalist candidate, was also there urging people to accept copies of a printed sheet he was distributing free.

Noisy

Throughout the meeting noisy shouting, heckling, and applause alternated. When the chairman of the Trades Council, Mr Joseph Duffy, closed the meeting there were still several people wanting to be heard.

The meeting opened with Mr Duffy dissociating the Trades Council from some of the solgans which had been shouted by marchers. He said: "We as a Trades Council are very much concerned about the unemployment situation in this town and we want all steps taken to have the unemployment situation solved.

"Nevertheless we as a Council wish to dissociate ourselves from some of the slogans and some of the shouts that were made in the demonstration. It is not the policy of this Trades Council to have Harold Wilson or the Labour Party out." He added: "We do not think the Conservative Party would do any better. The Conservatives would be infinitely worse."

Mr Dan McGarvey, President of the Boilermakers' Society, who was the main speaker at the meeting, urged the Wear's shipbuilding employers to move as fast as the unions in implementing the Geddes Report on the industry.

The unions, he said, had accepted the report, "We have pledged our co-operation to make the industry viable and we have done all sorts of things in relation to productivity agreements. We have moved faster than any union in any industry to get agreement with the employers.

"But the employers have not moved as fast as the union. We find the employers keep wrangling among themselves in relation to who is going to lose his job, when amalgamation comes about. We have the luxury of them wrangling over the financial situation of their jobs."

Mr McGarvey also said the Government should make up its mind about the proposed power station at Seaton Carew. "If it's

(Continued in Page 9)

—"Now to get on with the job"

FOLLOWING a busy round of interviews and introductions after his appointment yesterday afternoon, as reported in our later editions, Sunderland's new manager, Mr Alan Brown, started his second term of office with the club this morning, when he was formally introduced to his staff by the club vice chairman, Mr Jack Cooke.

In many cases it was a reunion with players and staff who had served under him in his previous tour of duty, but for others it was a first acquaintance with the man whom Sunderland have selected to guide them through the last, crucial stages of a battle to stave off the threat of relegation.

Afterwards, he lunched with the players at a seafront hotel before getting down to the task of plotting the plan of campaign for this afternoon's game against F.A. Cup-holders Tottenham Hotspur at Roker Park.

Mr Brown, whose surprise appointment had its starting point in direct talks between the Sunderland Chairman, Mr Syd Collings, and the Sheffield Wednesday Chairman, Dr Andrew Stephen, showed all his old facility for keeping questions within due bounds when he attended a Press conference immediately after his appointment.

"HAPPY WITH TERMS"

When yesterday's "guesstimates" that the job would carry a salary of £10,000 or £12,000 were mentioned, he said: "On my way up I saw newspaper contents bills naming a figure and I was absolutely staggered. This was madness."

Refusing to comment on salary or contract, he said: "I don't discuss club business in public. People who know me know that I do not bargain. I am happy with the terms. I am content."

Answering the suggestion that one of his reasons for leaving

By ARGUS

the club last time was that there had been rows, he said: "Of course there were differences of opinion here and there, but there were also very wide areas of agreement."

"TROUBLED CLUB"

He had heard this mentioned before, but said: "You should remember that Sunderland

[Continued in Back Page]

ANOTHER M.P. DIES

LABOUR M.P. for Brightside, Sheffield, since 1950, Mr Richard Emanuel Winterbottom, died today at his Sheffield home. He was 68.

His death means that eight by-elections are now pending—three of them in seats where Labour had majorities under 5,000. And Mr Francis Noel-Baker, Labour M.P. for Swindon, announced yesterday that he would resign at a time which would "suit general convenience."

Mr Winterbottom's death follows that of Mr Sydney Silverman, Labour M.P. for Nelson and Colne, yesterday.

The six by-elections in Labour seats will be at Acton (1966 majority 4,941), Brightside (19,177), Dudley (10,022), Meriden (4,581), Nelson (4,577), Oldham West (7,572). The two in Conservative seats are: South Kensington (14,631) and Warwick and Leamington (8,697).

Airstrip is reopened

NORTH VIETNAMESE gunners today temporarily cut off Khe Sanh base from the rest of South Vietnam by blowing up a fuel transport plane on the airstrip, but air supplies were resumed a few hours later.

A U.S. military spokesman said the fully-laden C-130 transport plane was hit by ground fire and exploded as it landed on the airstrip at the remote U.S. marine base in the north of the country, but the airstrip was cleared this afternoon.

The spokesman said two people were killed, four injured and three are missing. The four engined plane, workhorse of the Vietnam war, normally carries a crew of five and the identity of the passengers has not been established.

Sophia's denial

Sophia Loren today denied rumours reported in Italian newspapers that she had had another miscarriage. "I am upset, particularly upset," by the reports. "They are not true, they are without any foundation whatever," the actress told the Italian news agency ANSA by phone from her Swiss chalet near Lucerne.

RESCUED FROM FREIGHTER

TWENTY-FOUR people were rescued today from the stricken Canadian freighter Charney, adrift in the storm-swept North Atlantic, 550 miles east of Cape Hatteras, North Carolina.

The 22 crewmen and the only two passengers, a married couple, abandoned the 2,068-ton vessel after the ship's master radioed last night that he thought she might sink in a matter of hours.

LISTING HEAVILY

The U.S. Coast Guard said the Norwegian bulk freighter Vinni picked up the crew and two passengers from two life boats in the eight-foot high seas.

The Charney was reported to be listing heavily. Earlier the captain had said he was prepared to stay aboard the ship himself, but his 21-man crew would have to take to the life-rafts.

The Sultan of Perak State today opened the £20 million Batang Padang hydro-electric scheme in the Northern Cameron Highlands.

WOMAN DOCTOR FOUND HANGED

An Indian woman doctor whose daughter died suddenly last night was found hanging from a curtain fixture at her Shrewsbury flat today. She was Dr Roshan Ara Ashraff (27), who was on the staff at Shelton Mental Hospital, Shrewsbury. Last night her three-month-old child was taken to the Royal Salop Infirmary, Shrewsbury, where she was found to be dead.

Industrial action and the manager's job at Sunderland AFC dominated the headlines on 10th February 1968.

IT WAS IN 1968 ....

Dr Martin Luther King was shot and killed in Memphis

USSR invaded Czechoslovakia

The Post Office introduced the two tier postal system. First Class post cost 5p and Second Class 4p

The crisis in Northern Ireland began

London Bridge was sold, dismantled and re-built in Arizona, USA

Comedian Tony Hancock committed suicide leaving a note "Things seemed to go wrong too many times"

The Maxi car first took to the roads

The 5p coin was introduced

Cult television programme The Man From UNCLE came to an end

Russia sent an unmanned space ship around the moon

Congratulations by Cliff Richard was UK entry in the Eurovision Song Contest. It was voted into second position

Oliver won Best Picture category in Academy Awards

Prescription charges were introduced for the first time

The first manned Apollo mission was undertaken

Postcodes were used for the first time

Nixon was elected as US President

The I'm Backing Britain Campaign was launched

David Hemery won BBC Sports Personality Of The Year

The Trade Descriptions Act was introduced

The Beatles set up Apple Corps Ltd to promote 'Western Communism' only for it to fold within eight months with debts of £2 million

In Sunderland in 1968...

The end of an era came with the announcement that Sunderland's open air traders, affectionately known as 'Barrow Boys', were given notice to quit their pitches on a site at the edge of the new Market Square shopping development. No offer of an alternative site in the central area was forthcoming and as this was the only area in which the traders were interested, it seemed as if the Barrow Boys would disappear from Sunderland Town Centre by early 1969. A council spokesman said that the final break between the traders and Sunderland Corporation was not approved without regret as the Barrow Boys had been part of the town's character for many years.

Sunderland Corporation announced that all gas cookers were to be removed from the town centre's new sky scraper flats at Gilley Law and replaced by electric cookers. Six hundred tenants were affected by Government instructions to local authorities to examine tower blocks built on the Ronan Point system following a gas explosion and subsequent collapse of a tower block at Ronan Point in Canning Town, London. Seven tower blocks at Gilley Law were built on the same principal and several tenants were annoyed that their expensive gas cookers were being replaced by cheaper electrical models. One resident complained to the Sunderland Echo that her gas cooker cost £41 a year ago and now she was going to lose it and get fobbed off with a utility electric cooker worth £28. Another resident told a Sunderland Echo reporter, "Let the millionaires who built the flats pay for a deluxe electric cooker. Did we come out to Gilley Law to be robbed?"

Phoenix House was completed in 1968 by which time redevelopment work was progressing on the remainder of Union Street.

Many properties on the west side of Bridge Street were flattened in 1968 to accommodate the new inner ring road. A few days separate these two photographs. Soon afterwards, the Grand Hotel on the east side of the street and just visible on the upper photograph, would also be reduced to a pile of rubble.

On 8th February, Sunderland AFC manager Ian McColl issued the terse statement, "I have been relieved of my duties as from this moment and Alan Brown will be my successor." The news came less than an hour after Mr McColl had told Argus of the Sunderland Echo that he was announcing an unchanged team for Saturday's home game with Spurs. He had also just concluded the transfer deal which saw Scottish International Neil Martin move to Coventry City for a fee of £90,000. New manager Alan Brown's salary was reputed to be in the region of £10,000-£12,000, a figure which Argus commented would result in Sunderland being redubbed 'The Bank of England Club.'

More doom and gloom on the unemployment front came with the news that Hendon Rope Works was to close in June with the loss of 88 jobs. British Ropes, owners of the former Glaholm & Robson Factory, said that there would be a three month run down of production at Hendon before work was transferred to the company's factory at Retford in Nottinghamshire where production of small size ropes could be more economically manufactured. Production of Ropes on the Hendon site first started in 1857 and an international reputation was quickly established. By the 1920s, the Hendon factory was one of the country's biggest ropeworks and steel ropes for use in ships, mines, docks, shipyards and suspension bridges were made there. During World War Two, virtually every British Aircraft factory was supplied with Hendon Rope Wires.

Sunderland shipyards were warned that orders for five ships, worth an estimated £10 million, could be lost due to credit facilities being withdrawn by the Shipping Industry Board. The shipyards of Bartram & Sons, Joseph L Thompson and Sir James Laing were warned by the board that, because of the lack of progress in merging shipbuilding facilities on the River Wear in line with the Geddes Committee findings, it would no longer recommend the granting of credit facilities for ships built at their yards. Within weeks, the yards of Austin & Pickersgill and Bartram & Sons announced that they were to merge and in doing so they would bring together order books worth £15 million and a workforce of 2,000. Austin & Pickersgill would acquire the whole share capital of Bartram & Sons while the latter company would continue to trade under its own name. The two companies had worked closely together for some time, notably in the development of the Liberty ship replacement, the 15,000 ton SD14. The merger came only days after the Doxford & Sunderland Shipbuilding & Engineering Company had rejected proposals of either a merger or takeover of both Austin & Pickersgill and Bartram & Sons.

'A Backdoor To Nationalisation' was how the leader of the ruling Conservative Group on Sunderland Town Council described a tentative suggestion by the Ministry of Transport that the town's bus system should be merged into a Tyneside PTA. Councillor Stephenson told the Sunderland Echo that he would fight any Government attempt to take over Sunderland's Municipal Transport undertaking. Alderman Spain, chairman of the Transport Committee said that he was opposed to the idea of a PTA and certainly against any attempt to include Sunderland in a Tyneside based authority.

Sunderland Public Works Department started work on the first stage of the town's new inner ring road which would link Bridge Street with a new roundabout on the site of the Rose & Crown public house and the former Kennedy store at the junction of Gill Bridge Avenue and High Street West.

January 1968 and work would soon start on the construction of the new Civic Centre on this site.

National fame awaits Seaburn! That was the claim made by developers who hoped to persuade Sunderland Corporation to approve plans to lease the former Seaburn Golf Centre to American based Putt Putt Golf Courses. The Seaside Development Committee requested the General Purposes committee to recommend the lease of the property at a rental of £2,400 per year for a period of 21 years. This would be the first development of its type in Britain and project plans included a miniature 18 hole course with synthetic greens, miniature zoo, swimming pool, catering facilities and children's playground. Project approval was granted and Putt Putt opened on 19th July. Within four weeks, the 40 animal zoo was closed due to lack of interest.

It was announced in August that Washington had lost out to Cardiff in its bid to move the Royal Mint from London.

The Crown & Sceptre in Millfield was demolished in August as part of a general clearance of the area.

As decimal coins became legal tender on 23rd April, a Sunderland Echo reporter discovered that while most of the town's people interviewed knew of the new currency, few knew of the conversion value. An assistant in a Bridge Street tobacconists shop correctly handed the reporter 7½p change after being given 15p for a packet of ten cigarettes. However, few shoppers were immediately aware that the new 5p coin (at that time, the same size as a shilling) was equivalent in value to twelve old pennies.

Planning permission was granted for the conversion of the former Sans Street Mission into a cinema. Star Cinemas who at that time operated over 100 cinemas in the UK, proposed spending £60,000 to convert the building into a 700 seat cinema. Sans Street Mission was built in 1792 and included two preachers' houses, a vestry and a chapel keeper's dwelling. By 1807, the premises were found to be too small and a scheme for enlargement was embarked upon. The mission became a noteworthy stronghold for northern Methodism and was renowned for its work with children. By 1946, the cost of maintaining such large premises had become a problem and the mission finally closed in 1963. The conversion of the building into a cinema increased the number of cinemas in Sunderland to three; a far cry from the late forties when there were sixteen cinemas in the town. Of the thirteen to close since 1948, by 1968 five were functioning as bingo halls (Millfield, Plaza, Cora, Royal and Savoy), two had been converted into supermarkets (Marina and Regent), two had been demolished (Havelock and Picture House), while the Roker was in use as a garage, the Gaiety had been earmarked for flats and both the Palace and the Villiers were disused.

Sunderland's lone member of the I'm Backing Britain campaign worked an extra hour without pay at the Wear Glass Works of James A Jobling & Company Ltd. Charles Barker, 32, a fork lift truck driver finished the night shift at 7am rather than 6am after working an extra hour in the company's glassware stacking department where there was absenteeism due to illness. When interviewed by the Sunderland Echo, Mr Barker said he was not optimistic about the likelihood of other men in the factory following his example but he felt that some of the women might join in. "If everyone did it, we might get the country out of the red and pay less tax," said Mr Barker.

Further demolition in 1968 included properties in Bedford Street. By the time this photograph was taken, the Grand Hotel was living on borrowed time.

Sunderland Echo, Wednesday, November 20, 1968—9

THE IN-CROWD ARE HERE

NEW! NEW! NEW!
LATEST GREATEST EVER

IN SUNDERLAND
GREAT OPENING OF
CITY STYLISH
MODERN MENSWEAR SHOP
by **HERMAN** of Herman's Hermits

See the latest and greatest
in "IN FASHIONS" for men
Top names in Groovy
Gear direct from
London.

OPENS TOMORROW
12-30 p.m. approx.

SWINGING!

STYLE! STYLE! STYLE!

UP-TO-THE-MINUTE GEAR FOR YOU

DIRECT FROM LONDON—TOMORROWS STYLES

CITY STYLISH

UNION STREET, (Arcade) SUNDERLAND / Tel: 70282

Harry could choose from four Sunderland branches of TSB in 1968!

Lots of groovy, swinging gear (direct from London) was on sale at City Stylish when Peter Noone opened the shop on 21st November 1968.

Sunderland's Trustee Savings Bank reported one of the highest increases in deposits of any of the 78 branches in the country. Funds increased by 6.4 per cent (compared to the national average of 5.5 per cent) to £17,300,003. The bank's chairman commented, "Judging by our results, Wearside must be standing up to the economic squeeze better than people in other parts of the country." The bank also reported an encouraging increase in the number of new cheque accounts. When the service began in 1966, many customers regarded cheque accounts with suspicion but those people were now using the service with confidence.

Eleven Sunderland & District Social Clubs announced the formation of a caretaker committee to find ways of curbing rising entertainments costs. Bill Morgan secretary of Farringdon Social Club said that he aimed to set up an agency "To do what the Mecca and Bailey organisations do; bring good artists to the area at a fair price." Martin Collins of the DLI Club said, "We are getting absolutely robbed. We've got artists who were paid five shillings two or three years ago now asking for £30."

People who resolutely refused to take part in a mass migration from Sunderland's East End and chose to continue living there despite its deterioration during the sixties unveiled a plan to inject life into the area which they hoped might mean a return to the good old days. On 28th August, the Corporation's Planning Committee approved in principle a housing scheme for an area which had previously been scheduled for industrial development. The area, which had been waste land for over fifty years, was bordered by High Street East and Prospect Row. The residents who still lived there recalled the days when the East End was a hive of activity with dancing in the streets and on the Town Moor during long summer evenings. One resident even hoped for a revival of the East End carnival which was one of the post war period casualties.

Sunderland Corporation decided not to give financial support to the proposed North East Regional Open Air Museum at Beamish Hall. Seven local authorities had already pledged financial support and another was expected to do so, leaving Sunderland as the only local authority not to support the project.

Washington F Pit, the oldest working colliery in the country, announced that it was to close in June. Coal was first drawn from the pit in 1777. News of the closure followed the announcement that the colliery's Busty Seam had become exhausted. Work on the Brass Thill face was coming to an end and the pit, which was producing 13,000 tons of coal per day, would endeavour to re-locate as many of its 883 workforce as possible. The last shift clocked off at 5.30am on 21st June, thus ending 191 years of coal production. Productivity ran exceptionally high in the final months of the life of the pit which closed due to 'lack of reserves'. Mechanical mining was introduced at F Pit in 1950 and man power reached a peak figure of 1,540 workers in 1960.

The men of `F' Pit shortly before coal mining ceased at the site.

Sunderland Echo & Shipping Gazette

Echo
SUNDERLAND

No. 30,335 (96th YEAR)   FIVEPENCE
SATURDAY, APRIL 5, 1969

SIX O'CLOCK

THE TOWN HALL IS TO BE SOLD
Sunderland Civic Centre will release existing offices

SUNDERLAND Town Council will be recommended by the General Purposes Committee on Wednesday to instruct a firm of estate agents to dispose of the 79-year-old Town Hall, and its annexe, in Fawcett Street.

After considering the question of office accommodation which will become vacant when the new Civic Centre in Burdon Road is completed the Committee recommends that Messrs Hillier, Parker, May, and Rowden, be instructed to dispose of the Town Hall.

It also recommends that that the firm should be told to sub-instruct local firms of estate agents to dispose of other properties.

These include Athenaeum Buildings in Fawcett Street, at present occupied by the Borough Engineer's Department; 15 and 17 John Street, occupied by the Education and Welfare Departments; and Somerford Buildings and 40 Norfolk Street, occupied by the Children's and Weights and Measures Departments.

Also to be disposed of are 1, Toward Road, occupied by the Parks, Cemeteries, and Allotments Department, and Thornholme, in Thornholme Road, housing the Health Department, with the exception of the grounds which are required for road works.

Offer to union

The General and Municipal Workers Union, which may be contemplating the redevelopment of its premises at the junction of Athenaeum Street and Frederick Street, is to be asked if it is interested in acquiring 14 and 15 Frederick Street, occupied by the Building Inspectors' section of the Borough Engineer's Department. If the Union does not require the properties it is recommended they be disposed of through the sub-agents.

The Committee is recommending that Normanhurst, in Stockton Road, occupied by the Housing Department, and Grange House in Stockton Road, occupied by the Borough Architect's Department, be retained, but leased for a period not exceeding five years, as they may be the subject of major road proposals. It is recommended that Grange

Continued on Back Page.

"No Blue Riband bid for Q.E.2"

SIR BASIL SMALLPIECE, Cunard chairman, said today that reports from the liner Queen Elizabeth 2, now on her proving voyage, had been consistently good.

Sir Basil, speaking before flying to the Canary Islands to welcome the ship on her arrival at Teneriffe, said: "The many technical people on board have really put Q.E.2 through her paces.

"For the whole of the past four days, up to noon yesterday, she has averaged 30 knots. This is as much speed as the ship will ever need."

HAPPIER TRIP

Sir Basil added: "There is no question of Cunard going for the Blue Riband — those days have been overtaken by the aeroplane and will never return."

With him on his flight to the Canaries went Mr Anthony Hepper, chairman of Upper Clyde Shipbuilders, who built the liner.

The circumstances today were different from those when they last flew together to Teneriffe—last December, to meet a crippled Q.E.2 limping into port with turbine trouble.

Today, the liner was heading in fine style for the Canaries.

SUNDERLAND TOWN HALL.

RESORTS ENJOY BUMPER START TO THE HOLIDAY

LOCAL seaside traders as well as sun-starved holidaymakers were smiling in the sun again today and hoping the rest of the holiday holds out the promise of yesterday when Seaburn had its best Good Friday ever.

Spring sunshine following weeks of Arctic weather sparked off a lemming-like dash to the coast.

"A RECORD"

Sunderland's entertainment manager, Mr W. Holden, told the Echo today: "There is no doubt that yesterday's crowds were a record for Easter. The car park was full and the restaurants and amusement arcades reported substantial business."

Only a small number of people travelled out of the town, despite the fact that temperatures have been several degrees higher a short distance inland and are likely to remain so. At Sunderland railway station an official told the Echo "It has been a very quiet Easter."

AT CRIMDON

At Crimdon, too, the crowds were drawn to Easington R.D.C.'s holiday lido as if by a

magnet. After lunch extra staff had to be brought in to supplement the skeleton staff on duty for Easter.

Today the resort's manager, Mr Tom Reynolds, said: "Yesterday went very well indeed. It looks as though the weather will hold over the week-end and I am expecting a bumper beginning to the holiday season."

Elsewhere in the county the prospects of a sunny week-end brought motorists out in force again today.

"TAKE CARE"

But with the news of a big increase in the road toll so far, motoring organizations are urging: "Take meticulous care."

For many the Easter roads have been jams and bumper to bumper driving near coastal resorts.

At mid-day more than 900 cars on tour were travelling west into Wales along the M4 and more than 1,000 an hour in the eastern direction.

Steady traffic heading out of London in bright sunshine was reported to the A.A. A spokesman said: "About 25,000 vehicles an hour were leaving on the 25 main exit routes. This was less than at the same time yesterday but more than last Easter Saturday."

A HEART OF PLASTIC

A fibre and plastic heart today beat within a 47-year-old man after surgeons in Houston, Texas carried out the world's first total artificial heart transplant operation.

A team at St Luke's Hospital, led by Dr Denton Cooley, substituted the device for the heart of Mr Haskell Karp, of Skokie, Illinois, a printing estimator.

Mr Karp was in satisfactory condition with the device and the device would remain in his chest until a donor was found and a human heart transplant could be performed, a hospital spokesman said.

£25,000

The weekly £25,000 Premium Bond prize today was won by bond number

4VL 768068

The winner lives in Cornwall.

£70,000 gems raid

Armed raiders got rings worth about £70,000 after overpowering members of the staff at an Oxford Street, London, jewellers today. One, dressed as a postman, called at the back door of the jewellers, Michael Davis and Sons, and when a member of the staff opened the door, three men, one with a shotgun, rushed in and forced two other staff members to open a safe.

Road toll is down

THE road toll was down yesterday after Thursday's bad start to the Easter holiday — and the number of deaths over the two days was the same as last year, 34.

Ministry of Transport figures for the 24 hours ended midnight last night were: accidents, 650; deaths, 13; serious injuries, 227; slight injuries, 633.

For the corresponding period last year the figures respectively were: 661, 21, 249, 657.

Total numbers since midnight last Wednesday are now: accidents 1,266; deaths, 34; serious injuries, 441; slight injuries, 1,204. The figures for the corresponding period last year were 1,210, 34, 408, and 1,150.

Bid to block resolution on teachers' pay fails

AN attempt by the Executive of the National Union of Teachers to defeat a resolution calling for a new basic salary scale of £1,000 to £2,000 over ten years failed at the union's annual conference in Douglas today.

An amendment moved by Mr Miles Clark, chairman of the Salaries Committee, sought to have the structure of salary scales reviewed and fresh recommendations put before the 1970 conference. When it was put to the conference it was heavily defeated. Further amendments to the resolution will go before the conference when the salaries debate is resumed on Monday.

The resolution expressed discontent with the teachers' pay and called for a new salary policy that would include the new scale, the removal of primary differential and the abolition of the system of consolidated scales for head teachers.

It also instructed the executive that if negotiations fail to produce a satisfactory settlement, a special conference of the union be called to decide on further action.

The resolution came four days after the introduction of the pay settlement giving a basic scale over 14 years.

PILOTS' STRIKE OFF

THE six-day B.O.A.C. pilots' strike is over following peace talks in London lasting 23 hours.

The settlement was announced by Captain Laurie Taylor, chairman of the British Airline Pilots Association, and B.O.A.C.'s chief negotiator, Mr Jim Atherton, the airline's general manager for industrial relations this afternoon. No details of the agreement were announced and no date

was given for resumption of flights.

Captain Taylor declined to disclose details of the settlement until after it has been put before the Association's Executive Council and members, probably tonight.

Announcement of the settlement was made at the headquarters of the National Joint Council for Civil Air Transport where the almost non-stop negotiations had gone on since yesterday.

FOOTBALL HALF-TIMES

SUNDERLAND 1 ARSENAL 0
Bristol Rovers 0, Reading 1
Northampton 0, Plymouth 1
Aberdeen 3, Airdrie 0
Colchester 1, Exeter 0
Cowdenbeath 1, Montrose 1
Blackpool 1, Sheffield Utd 1
Motherwell 0, Stranraer 0
BRADFORD 1, DARLINGTON 2
Liverpool 1, Wolves 0
Halifax 0, Swansea 1
Southport 0, Rotherham 0
St Johnstone 0, Kilmarnock 0
Forfar 1, Queen of South 0
Stenhousemuir 1, Stirling Alb 0
Raith 0, Hearts 1
St Mirren 0, Dunfermline 1
Orient 1, Barrow 2
Watford 3, Crewe 0
Leeds 0, Manchester City 0
Tranmere 1, Oldham 1
Brechin 0, East Fife 2
Lincoln 3, Workington 0
Southend 0, Grimsby 0
Derby 2, Bolton 0
Manchester Utd 1, Notts Forest 1
Rochdale 0, York City 1
Notts County 2, Wrexham 0
STOCKPORT 1, HARTLEPOOL 0
Blackburn 0, Fulham 1
Sheff Wed 1, West Ham Utd 1

Latest

3.15—CARLISLE
1, Glen Abbey (20-1); 2, Sea Romance (10-1); 3, Flatbush (11-2). Fu. 15 ran.

3.30—KEMPTON
1, Be Friendly (10-11 f); 2, Star and Garter (100-30); 3, Great Pear (6-1).

3.30—DONCASTER
1, Renardier (10-1); 2, Galosh (9-1); 3, Humberside (100-8). F. un.

3.30—TEESSIDE
1, Lake District (4-1); 2, Batchelor (5-1); 3, Gabriel Grub (6-4 fav).

3.30—WARWICK
1, Piobair (7-4 f); 2, Pugilist (13-2); 3, Loot of India (33-1).

A bleak day for many Wearsiders. The decision to demolish Sunderland's once proud Town Hall is an emotive subject to this day.

IT WAS IN 1969 ...

Colour TV was launched on BBC 1 and ITV

The 50p coin was introduced

The voting age was lowered to 18

Troops were first sent to Northern Ireland

Concorde set off on its maiden flight

$^1/_2$d coin ceased to be legal tender

Neil Armstrong became the first man to set foot on the moon on July 21

Star Trek was first shown on BBC TV — on moon landing day

John Lennon returned his MBE

Woodstock concert took place. The event lasted 60 hours and attracted an estimated 450,000 people thus becoming the biggest youth happening of the decade

Boom-Bang-A-Bang by Lulu was the UK entry in the Eurovision Song Contest. It was voted into joint first place together with three other songs

Midnight Cowboy won Best Picture Category in Academy Awards

Ann Jones won BBC Sports Personality Of The Year

Ford announced the arrival of their new Capri car

The total US death toll in the Vietnam War was given as 33,630 to date which was more than the total killed in the entire Korean War

The final episode of radio serial The Dales was broadcast. The programme was originally broadcast as Mrs Dale's Dairy

Monty Python's Flying Circus was first shown on BBC 2 on October 5

In Sunderland in 1969...

Dr M. Hutton, rector of Sunderland Polytechnic expressed the opinion that qualified people should be offered more money to work in Sunderland, "Because the town's general impression of grey mediocrity failed to attract sufficient applicants for jobs." Speaking at a conference on the future of Sunderland in Wearmouth Hall, Dr Hutton said that the North East may not attract many top people but Sunderland attracted none at all.

At the Pallion factory of Electrosil, 170 strikers were dismissed during May. Production at the factory which manufactured resistors and micro-electronic equipment was brought to a standstill during the strike which it was estimated, cost the company £100,000 in lost production. Workers claimed that factory management were refusing to consider pay and productivity proposals unless skilled workers were downgraded to semi-skilled status. The company subsequently withdrew the dismissal notices and agreed to abandon the new conditions of employment which were at the heart of the strike.

Colin Suggett, Sunderland's 20 year old inside forward, was sold to West Bromich Albion for £100,000.

News that came as a relief to Wearsiders was that it would cost nothing to use Sunderland's public conveniences after decimalisation. The Highways Committee revealed that the cost of replacing or converting locks on toilet doors would be £2,500.

As soon as Sunderland's new inner ring road scheme was approved The Rose and Crown's days were numbered. Today, the road passes through the site formerly occupied by the pub which was demolished in 1969.

A new traffic system, which dispensed with the need for a roundabout, was introduced at the Durham Road/Barnes Park Road junction in 1969.

8th November saw the disappearance of a familiar Sunderland landmark as the Roker Baths Road bridge which carried the mineral line to the docks was demolished.

A spectacular fire in Sunderland town centre brought fire engines racing into town from neighbouring areas as twelve appliances fought the blaze at the furniture store of Adrian Share in Bridge Street. As police threw up road blocks around the area, the fire threatened to spread to all other shops on the block. Police stood by as proprietors of adjoining shops removed goods including fur coats and television sets from their premises. As the blaze spread from the second to the third floor of the furniture store, part of the flooring collapsed. With Bridge Street still closed the following morning, there was traffic chaos in the town centre. The building was in such a bad state that the shell was later demolished. Two 12-year-old boys were later charged with starting the fire.

Austin & Pickersgill announced orders for ten SD14 cargo motor ships and one 15,000 ton cargo liner, worth a total of £13 million. The news meant that the River Wear had received orders for fifteen SD14s (the replacement for the Liberty ship) during 1969. The year was a good one for the five River Wear shipyards with a post war output record of 291,484 gross tons of shipping being produced. It was the highest tonnage since 1943 and beat the previous best post war return of 283,160 tons. The Wear easily topped the North East coast shipbuilding league being well ahead of the Tyne (214,530 tons) and the Tees (75,102 tons).

INTRODUCTION OF ZONAL FARE SYSTEM

4ᴰ CASH ANY ZONE (OR PART ZONE) OR 1 TOKEN
CHILDREN AND CONCESSIONARY PASS HOLDERS 3ᴰ ANY DISTANCE

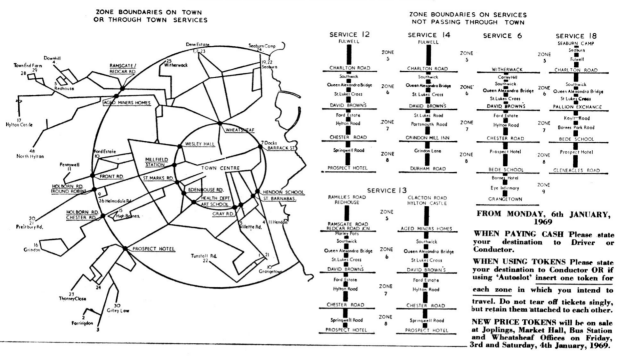

FROM MONDAY, 6th JANUARY, 1969

WHEN PAYING CASH Please state your destination to Driver or Conductor.

WHEN USING TOKENS Please state your destination to Conductor OR if using 'Autoslot' insert one token for each zone in which you intend to travel. Do not tear off tickets singly, but retain them attached to each other.

NEW PRICE TOKENS will be on sale at Joplings, Market Hall, Bus Station and Wheatsheaf Offices on Friday, 3rd and Saturday, 4th January, 1969.

In January 1969, Sunderland Corporation replaced the flat fare system on its buses with a zonal system, the details of which it advertised in the Sunderland Echo.

In 1969 Gaytours meant nothing more than a 'Happy-Go-Luxury Holiday'!

A housewive's dream come true in popular two tone colours.

This most majestic of buildings, The Grand Hotel, had fifty bedrooms and a popular public bar. It closed for business in 1969 and was demolished shortly afterwards.

The green light was given to a £3 million Wearside sports scheme. The plans comprised a £1 million sports and recreational centre to be built between Crowtree Road and The Green. The centre would house two large sports courts, a gymnastic court, shop, cafe, discotheque, club room and a lecture hall. Work could start during 1970/1971. Other plans included a sports stadium at Barnes Park, a 100 acre outdoor site at Doxford Park, a town centre ice rink and two small sports centres. A subsequent report which was published on 1st October recommended that the multi-purpose recreation centre should be built on a 3.75 acre site at Crowtree Road adjacent to the new shopping centre. The revised cost was given as £1.5 million with a target open date as early 1973. The report said that the site had been chosen as the most easily accessible by bus and train and there were also good parking facilities in the area. The construction of the building would form a natural extension to the re-vitalisation of the heart of the town and would assist in developing Sunderland into a 'city type centre'.

Not quite so spoilt for choice! Dee Time, Rolf Harris or Eurovision Song Contest.

Spoilt for choice! Pink Floyd, The Coasters, Love Affair or Karl Denver Trio.

It was a matter for pleasure that Sunderland had not been chosen by the Government as one of the towns in which hard gaming was to be allowed, said Alderman Cohen at a meeting of Sunderland's Protection Committee on 18th November. He was responding to a petition signed by 1,783 patrons of Wetherells Club who deplored any attempt to restrict facilities on the premises. Alderman Cohen said he was not against someone having a bet on a horse but it was his view that hard gaming on the tables could lead to "vice, oppression and thuggery".

November 20th saw in excess of 1,400 teachers march on the Sunderland Education Department offices in what was claimed to be the most massive display of trade union solidarity on Wearside in post war years. The demonstration was called jointly by the National Union of Teachers and the National Association of Schoolmasters in support of a pay claim. Thousands of shoppers, office workers and children on holiday from the town's strike bound schools lined the route of the procession which stretched a quarter of a mile from Park Lane to John Street. Following the half day strike, the teachers returned to their classrooms.

seven minute sprint from Roker Park (if you can keep up with Colin Todd)

Sunderland's football team in their kit   Sunderland's football team in our kit.

This advertisement appeared in The Sunderland Echo on 12th March 1969 and shows the Sunderland AFC first team squad of the day.

Many Wearsiders were saddened on 23rd January to see scaffolding going up around the Rose & Crown public house at the corner of High Street West and Gill Bridge Avenue and the adjoining, former Kennedy's Cobden Exchange in readiness for their demolition. Both buildings were making way for the new inner ring road system.

A £21 million merger was agreed by the boards of Sunderland Building Society and the Corporation & Eligible Building Society of South Shields. It was announced that the merged society would be named Sunderland & South Shields Building Society and would be operational from 1st July. It would be the second biggest North East based building society.

Mr R. E. Bottrill, manager of Sunderland Corporation Transport left the undertaking to take up a similar position in Portsmouth. His reported new salary of £4,065 per annum was marginally more than he was paid at Sunderland. His parting comment was: "The Sunderland public want a taxi service with bus fare rates and obviously this is not practicable."

89

Three of Sunderland's oldest family motor businesses Dunn's Garages, Byers Garages and Turvey & Co — merged their operations in September. Turvey's first started trading in Sunderland during 1880 while both Dunn's and Byers were established in 1919. All three dealers dealt solely in British cars over the years and, at the time of the merger, all handled vehicles from the then recently formed Leyland Motors Corporation. The merged business was known as Byers, Dunn, Turvey Group Ltd and commenced operations with an annual turnover of £3 million.

Sunderland Corporation began the unusual job of investigating one of its own publications to see if it was breaking the law! A two page colour advertisement in the town's holiday brochure invited visitors to Seaburn Hall Variety Club to be entertained by stars of stage, screen, television and radio. Plans for Seaburn Hall Variety Club had been shelved months earlier and it appeared that no one had attempted to cancel the brochure advertisement. One Seaburn trader told the Sunderland Echo: "I think it is a disgrace. People up and down the country are being led up the garden path and are naturally annoyed to discover there is no club." In his foreward to the brochure, the Chairman of the Recreation Committee commented: "Seaburn Hall has been taken over by a firm of amusement caterers who are sparing no expense in turning the hall into one of the most luxurious variety clubs in the North East." Another brochure advertisement described the Empire Theatre's summer season as offering the best in popular and classical entertainment with top class companies from Britain and abroad offering drama, ballet and music of excellence. In reality the Empire's 1969 summer season consisted of a season of films!

Customers at Presto's town centre supermarket laughed as they watched thieves take bundles of bank notes from an open safe in the store. The haul, believed to be worth £500, was watched by around 40 customers who stood laughing as one of the two men involved in the theft scaled a partition wall into an office where a safe had been left open, while his accomplice kept a lookout. One customer actually recognised one of the thieves but refused to identify him, saying: "Good luck to them if they can do it in daylight and get away with it." In response, the store manager commented: "This seems to be the general attitude of the public."

The 1969 decision of vandalism to demolish Sunderland's beloved Town Hall had this end result by 1971.

Going ...   *Going ...*   *Gone.*

A must for Sunderland Historians!

THE BUSES OF SUNDERLAND CORPORATION TRANSPORT *1929-1973*

From 1929 until 1973, Sunderland Corporation operated its own fleet of motor buses. For most of those years, car ownership was much lower than it is today and Sunderland residents relied largely upon public transport to get them around the town; whether it be to work, to the shops, to the seaside or a night out. The fares were virtually the cheapest in the country.

The earliest buses were painted chocolate and cream although this was changed in the early thirties and to red and cream and again in the early fifties to green and cream.

By 1954, the last tram had run in Sunderland and the bus fleet then expanded dramatically.

The book traces the development and expansion of Sunderland through its bus fleet. As the boundaries of the town expanded, so did its bus routes to carry people to their homes. A comparison of Sunderland Corporation's list of bus routes in 1939, 1953 and 1960 is a fascinating exercise.

In 1966, Sunderland Corporation became the first transport undertaking in Britain to operate a flat fare system on its buses. One man operated, single deck buses were introduced at this time to replace the older double deck buses.

The book includes over seventy photographs of Sunderland's buses at work in areas of bygone Sunderland.

> *Do you remember:-*
◆ Universal tickets
◆ The Circle route
◆ The 'Little Bus' which ran from Grangetown to Town and Grangetown to Southwick and pioneered Pay As You Enter bus operation in Sunderland
◆ Clippies
◆ Bus Tokens
◆ The Promenade Tour

The Buses of Sunderland Corporation Transport is available from Sunderland Echo outlets, good bookshops or direct from Mel Kirtley by sending a cheque for £4.95 to PO Box 19, Washington, Tyne and Wear, NE37 2AT.
Cheques payable to: Mel Kirtley.

READ ALL ABOUT IT!

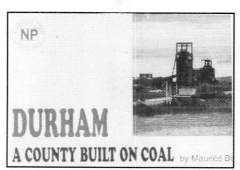

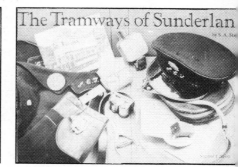